HIS WAY

BY JAMES W. TAYBURN

TRILOGY

His Way

Trilogy Christian Publishers A Wholly Owned Subsidary of Trinity Broadcasting Network

2442 Michelle Drive Tustin, CA 92780

Copyright © 2023 by James W. Tayburn

Cover design by: Natalee Groves

For information about special discounts for bulk purchases, please contact Trilogy Christian Publishing.

Manufactured in the United States of America

10 9 8 7 6 5 4 3 2 1

Library of Congress Cataloging-in-Publication Data is available.

ISBN: 979-8-88738-239-5

E-ISBN: 979-8-88738-240-1

DEDICATION

This book is dedicated to my Heavenly Father, who was running after me even when I was running away. Colossians 3:23 (NIV) says, "Whatever you do, work at it with all your heart, as working for the Lord, not for human masters." That makes all the difference in what my priorities are today.

TABLE OF CONTENTS

INTRODUCTION

For about thirty years, I've been writing poetry and have, at times, been mesmerized by the power of a good poem to touch the human spirit and bring people to tears. When this happens, I become even more certain that a poet's words, the ups and downs of life, and God's presence are all interconnected. As I've made it my daily habit to study God's Word, learning more of what He wants from me, I believe more of my poetry has been Holy Spirit-inspired.

I lived much of my life as an atheist, and many years passed before I was able to "stumble into enlightenment," accept Jesus as my Lord and Savior, and be born again. Without an extraordinary helping of amazing grace, there would have been no hope for me. There are a lot of things I don't do well, but God has given me the gift of creating poetry, and my mission is to bring people to His Kingdom with the words He gives me. It is said that if our God-given talent leads one person to accept Christ as their Savior, it's worth the effort, and I certainly agree.

There are over a hundred poems in this book, but my hope would be that you find that one or two that have special meaning for you. Each poet has a personal style; mine is that each poem is built on rhyme, delivers a message for life, and, most important, honors God. Life is a journey, and I pray, whether you read this book in one sitting or as a daily devotional, that it is a journey that brings you closer to the Lord.

Creation—Nature

"The heavens declare the glory of God; the skies proclaim the work of his hands. Day after day they pour forth speech; night after night they reveal knowledge. They have no speech, they use no words; no sound is heard from them. Yet their voice goes out into all the earth, their words to the ends of the world" (Psalm 19:1–4, NIV).

A GREAT BIG GOD

When it comes to knowledge, man tends to beat his own drum
And the accomplishments have been impressive, one by one
Replacing body organs, once thought to be impossible
Robotic surgeries done with precision beyond plausible

Digital technology that seems to be growing with no limit
Tasks that used to take days are done in less than a minute
Cars so sophisticated they can drive themselves anywhere
Someone half a world away conducting modern warfare

Lest our heads swell too much and we think we're in control
Let's consider the view of the One who owns our soul
Psalm 19 says, "The heavens declare God's glory"
The work of His hands tells us the complete story

So, let's take a look at the Universe our great God created
And see if we still think His sovereignty is overstated
The sun in our small Milky Way Galaxy is 94 million miles away
And we haven't come close to traversing this celestial highway

In one year, light travels over 5 trillion miles; that's beyond quick
Referred to as a light year, it's our astrophysicists' measuring stick
Now consider that the diameter of our Milky Way is 100,000 light years
And there may be 100 billion other galaxies in our space frontier

That in itself is incredible, but it's only one way to look at God's creation
The size of the Universe will exceed even the wildest imagination
At 15 billion light years wide, it certainly qualifies as the edge of infinity
And the precision movement of each body verifies the hand of divinity

God's thoughts are not our thoughts, even if they're from the heart
When you look at His creation, they're 15 billion light years apart
If you dwell on these special distances for just a minute, you'll be awed
We can stop thinking we're in control and begin serving a great big God.

BODY, MIND, AND SOUL

We hear a lot about body, mind, and soul
The three parts of each of us that make us whole
And man has learned much about the first two
But about the third, we're still without a clue

Great strides have been made in how the body works
There's a pill for just about every kind of hurt
Almost every part of the body can be replaced
Medical knowledge advancing at a frenetic pace

Diseases that were once the scourge of society
Have been nearly eliminated from our vocabulary
Even diseases like cancer and those of the heart
Are no longer the death sentence they were at the start

And we seem to be unlocking some mysteries of the brain
Surgeries thought impossible are performed again and again
We're learning how we learn and how we forget
Where our emotions come from—anger, love, and regret

We're beginning to see how mind and body work together
To make this living, breathing organism function better
The brain is a very complex computer, and overseeing mentor
Body parts respond to the instruction of this control center

But what about that third element, the one we call soul?
Considered to be the center of choice and self-control
Why can't we locate it anywhere in the body physique?
If it's the one thing that makes each of us unique

We know without it, the body stops functioning and dies
Yet, we cannot find where this vital part lies
All of the body parts are still there, but now they don't work
Because what makes us "us" has departed from this earth

This is the one part of "us" medicine or science cannot explain
And there's a good reason why what we know is not germane
It's the spiritual hub that our Creator placed in each of us
And it makes us who we are, in whom or what we put our trust

There are so many things from God not completely understood
But He did promise that there is a day coming when we would
That when we die, He reclaims that part of us we know as soul
And we move on to another dimension of existence, another fold

We can't see our soul just like we can't see heaven
It's one of the mysteries God chooses to keep hidden
But it's our lifeline, the connector between us and Him
If that connector is broken, we're doomed to a life of sin

A church without believers is just a building, dead
But filled with believers, it's very much alive instead
So it is with our bodies; without souls, they die
And while on Earth, we'll just never understand why

As hard as it may be, the soul is to be honored the most
It's the receptor given to us by our Lord and heavenly host
It's our spiritual lifeline telling us what we should be
And it's our key to a life with Him in eternity

There's a whole spiritual world we just cannot see
But it's more real than the starkest reality
And there's only one connection to it; it's called soul
While not understood, it's what makes us whole.

FOLLOW THE LIGHT

Where do we go today when we want answers to almost anything?
Don't we just fire up our computers and consult with the Google king?
Early man didn't have the benefit of the iPad or the iPhone
But he understood so much more completely we're not alone

He knew that God provided the answers if we just looked to the sky
The timeless questions of the meaning of life—the who, what, and why
From the very beginning, man knew that evil lurked in the dark
But also knew that God could shine a light into each man's heart

On the first day of creation, God said let there be light, and there was
It was called day when light prevails and night when darkness does
The sun provided all that was needed, warmth and comfort each day
But it was in the darkness that we stumbled and lost our way

God sent the sun, but He also sent His Son to light our path
Jesus obeyed His Father's will and took the punishment on our behalf
His light shines brighter than any sun or any cavalcade of stars
And it's only through Him we discover why we're here and who we are

Let's be clear; there's a lot of darkness everywhere we look
And the answers are not going to be found in some self-help book
But if you just follow Jesus' example, you'll be doing all right
The answers are there; look to the heavens and follow the light.

GOD-MAN OR GOO-MAN?

Are we the result of a random series of events or made by God?
Is it to Darwin's theory of evolution or to creation we give the nod?
Do we really believe we're descended from the amoeba or paramecium?
Or do we owe everything to the Creator and His risen Son?

Did God breathe life into Adam, as the Bible says, on dry land?
Or did we simply emerge from the swamp as a kind of goo-man?
How do we answer the difficult questions of life for you and I?
Who am I, why am I here, and what happens to me when I die?

If it was seventy fallen leaves, all in a perfect row, you were seeing
Would you attribute it to happenstance or an intelligent being?
So why do we continue to doubt what's written in the Good Book?
The answers are all there, including creation, if we just look

If you doubt there being a Creator, I suggest you look to the sky
Embrace it like a child who stares at it in wonder and wide-eye
Why is there such order to every body in the Universe that we see?
How can a computer identify, at any point in time, where each will be?

How can we even fathom forever or conceptual infinity
When we can't even reach the limits of our own galaxy?
That there are a billion more is just beyond imagination
And yet, somehow, we cannot embrace the thought of creation

There's the human body, an amazing machine of such complexity
That at the cellular level, we see astounding order and biochemistry
Mechanisms at work so intriguing they take away our breath
When we cut our finger, for instance, why don't we bleed to death?

So, whether we look outward or inward, the conclusion's the same
He's the Almighty, the Creator, the name to place above all names
It's to Him we are to render all obedience, devotion, and trust
His commandments are not just a good idea; they're a must

Why is it that man keeps looking in the box for philosophical clues?
And tries to generalize the particulars to a universal worldview
When the universals are all right there for us to read and understand
If we just accept that God sits outside the box, with our fate in His hand

The Bible says God created, in His own image, mankind
Do you think it was a random goo-man He had in mind?
Is it all about us, as Maslow would say, that we self-actualize
Or should we be concerned about how we look in the Creator's eyes?

God showed us in the Garden that He's a jealous god, *El Qanna*
He expects that we will worship Him in reverence and awe
Not put Him in the box and decide to go our own way
As our secular society seems determined to do today

So what's it going to be? Are we going to bow down to The One?
And give all to the Father, the Holy Spirit, and the Son
Or are we going to believe what's in the box, proven a sham
I don't know about you, but I'm not betting my eternity on the goo-man.

MOUNTAIN MOODS

I went to the mountains; only emptiness there
Hawks and their buddies had flown south somewhere
Animals along the ground had departed for water and food
And the mountain was engrossed in a somber mood

I went to the mountains; snow covered its peaks
In the quiet of the moment, nature still speaks
Crisp, clean air permeates my waiting lungs
And my soul is hostage to the glistening sun

I went to the mountains, black as could be
Dark and foreboding robbed my security
Uneasiness settles over that sinister mount
As if some unseen calamity is about to play out

I went to the mountains; nothing could I see
A foggy mist sequesters its ridges in canopy
This ghastly shroud stokes my latent fears
And I'm comforted when it finally clears

I went to the mountains, ominous clouds on high
Lightning, God's laser show, arcs across the sky
Thunder jolts me from my stuporous trance
First raindrops strike the rocks and dance

I went to the mountains, feeling quite low
But my spirit was lifted by a double rainbow
No matter how troublesome or challenging the day
Rainbows are God's promise that all is okay

I went to the mountains, clothed in emerald green
Watched plants spring to life and animals preen
Listened carefully and heard the refrain
Of nature's joyous acceptance of monsoon rain

I went to the mountains, golden in drape
Saguaros step out from the desert landscape
Rocks acquire a luster with the evening light
Afternoon's radiant showcase gives way to the night

I went to the mountains, Beethoven there
Hawks and turkey vultures float on a carpet of air
It's nature's symphony played out before our eyes
As they dip below the horizon, then catch a thermal and rise

I went to the mountains, clouds all apuff
Fill my senses with their winsome fluff
They hang there on the cliffs, attached it seems
It's a magical time, and it fuels my dreams

I went to the mountains in the darkness of night
A silhouette against the sky, reflecting power and might
A billion stars captivate the setting as only they can
A full moon perches on the ridge as if placed there by hand

I go to the mountains, sometimes only in mind
As I extend my gaze upward, here's what I find
Each interlude is different, always mesmerizing and new
And I say, "Thank You, Lord, for this magnificent view."

THE ANSWER'S IN YOUR BACKYARD

Are you someone who just can't accept the idea of creation?
That there has to be some kind of humanistic explanation
That, somehow, all the right stuff randomly came together
And complex DNA strands were formed without a director

Look around at the interconnected structure of nature today
Could a random series of events have really set it up that way?
Isn't it more plausible that it's the result of some intelligent design?
That all the pieces were carefully crafted by some superior mind

The answer to this age-old question might be in your own yard
Take a look around at the wonders; you won't have to go far
A perfect time to contemplate all of this is at the onset of Spring
When God does His absolute best to showcase everything

Isn't it amazing that everything a plant requires is in one seed?
That in that one tiny element is all the information it will ever need
To sprout, to grow, and to become whatever it was meant to be
And to beautify our world in ways astounding to believe

Take a stroll around your backyard and note the wonders you see
Buds develop, and flowers open in this springtime jubilee
The colors encompass every hue and shade of the rainbow
And what causes their delicate petals to unfold, no one knows

The types of flowers are as varied as the imagination can conceive
Roses, lantana, lilac, lupine—just a few of the thousands you'll see
Even the prickly desert cactus puts on its own kind of show
With great big beautiful blossoms, they're able to bestow

Notice how the bees gather at the flowers to fulfill their mandate
And in satisfying their desire for nectar, help the plants pollinate
Hummingbirds, in their probing for nectar, do exactly the same
God put these intricacies together so it would glorify His name

Nature is an intricate web of plants, animals, insects, and birds
The way it all fits together makes the idea of happenstance absurd
Everything seems coordinated in accord with some master plan
And how anyone could think this was random is hard to understand

So question if all this was created by God if you must
But if you just look around, your mindset will have to adjust
You won't have to study biology or even walk that far
Sit on your patio and observe; the answer's in your backyard.

THE GOD ZONE

Rod Serling famously introduced us every week to "The Twilight Zone"
It was, as he described it, a place between shadow and light,
Between science and superstition, between the known and unknown
A dimension of space and infinity of neither day nor night

Serling's "Twilight Zone" was a place of the weird and bizarre
A place where man was incapable of understanding events
We didn't know which direction our mind had traveled to or how far
A dimension we could not fathom from any previous experience

While Twilight Zone centered around man's cognitive limitations
And our inability to grasp extended parameters of time and space
There's another zone beyond even Rod Serling's keen imagination
Heaven, yes—but The God Zone is how we'll refer to this place

The God Zone is a place where those great questions get answers
Where we'll be made aware of God's perfect plan in all its glory
Where we'll celebrate with joy like the ballroom dancer
And that peace beyond all understanding will cap the story

Much has been written about the picture heaven will paint
That we'll have new bodies and sickness will be no more
There will be no more tears, no more sorrow for these saints
Eternity with the Father and Son will be like nothing before

Rod Serling was not a Christian but had a wild imagination
In wondering what was out there in space, he was not alone
But Christians know with certainty what lies beyond the constellations
And that one day, we'll cross over and live forever in The God Zone.

THE OLIVE TREE

There are so many amazing creations of our God
Just stand still, look around, and be awed
The mountains that rise up out of the plain
The cactus that can live with virtually no rain

The stars and planets, all moving in synchronization
In a pattern that's remained the same since creation
How the animals have adapted in order to stay alive
The bees who are the key to how most plants survive

Then there's us; the most intricate earthly being stands alone
A living complex of veins, arteries, nerves, muscle, and bone
All systems controlled by the master computer, the brain
And how it all works together, no one can really explain

We could pick out any organism now living on earth
And extol its virtues; what it does to present its worth
The candidates would be plenty, but you may not believe
If I ask you to consider the case of the olive tree

The olive tree has stood the test of time, longevity
Two-thousand-year-old versions stand in the Garden of Gethsemane
There when Christ was betrayed by a treacherous heart
And it was an olive branch the dove brought back to the ark

The symbolism of the olive tree can be a guide in our faith
So many messages to show us how to live for Christ's sake
Among other things, it's an international sign of peace
A signal to lay down arms, start talking, and all conflict cease

The steadfastness and perseverance of the olive tree are hard to refute
After years of drought, heat, and storms, it's still producing fruit
While its trunk and its bark may be gnarled and twisted
It is to be applauded for all the various attacks it's resisted

Admirable characteristics even for us—challenged but still resolute
We may be old and gnarly, but that shouldn't stop us from producing fruit
And to everyone around us, couldn't we just bring an aroma of peace?
Offering in our attitude an olive branch, all animosity released

The olive tree is able to survive by sending its roots deep
Grabbing nutrients and water other trees cannot reach
We, too, as Christians, can survive in much the same way
Developing roots that go deep and connect to our Lord every day

The fruit of the olive tree produces oil when it's pressed
Oil that's treasured for food and health benefits it may possess
Likewise, Jesus was crushed, and His blood poured out on the cross
And that blood is treasured as the way to the Father for the lost

So you see, the olive tree provides us with quite a metaphor
For how we're to live out our lives; what we're here for
And regardless of our age, we can still accomplish good
Producing the good fruit that God always thought we could.

HOPE—REFLECTION

"'For I know the plans I have for you,' declares the Lord, 'plans to prosper you and not harm you, plans to give you hope and a future" (Jeremiah 29:11, NIV).

"Finally, brothers and sisters, whatever is true, whatever is noble, whatever is right, whatever is pure, whatever is lovely, whatever is admirable— if anything is excellent or praiseworthy—think about such things" (Philippians 4:8, NIV).

A Poet's Rendition of Ecclesiastes 3

There's a time under heaven for everything
And each season will a new life circumstance bring
A time to laugh and a time to cry
A time to be born and a time to die

A time for sitting out and a time to dance
A time for work and a time for romance
A time for holding back and a time to be bold
A time for youth and a time for old

A time to be strong and a time to be weak
A time to be silent and a time to speak
A time for business and a time to retire
A time to lay back and a time to inspire

A time for water and a time for wine
A time for the physical and a time for divine
A time to walk and a time to run
A time to be serious and a time for fun

A time for strangers and a time for friends
A time to save and a time to spend
A time for the rich and a time for the poor
A time for less and a time for more

A time to stand tall and a time to take a knee
A time for discipline and a time to be free
A time to stay and a time to roam
A time for gathering and a time to be alone

A time to receive and a time to give
A time to admonish and a time to forgive
There's a time under heaven for God's perfect plan
And the plan will be unique for every woman and man.

A Poet's Rendition of the 23rd Psalm

The Lord is my shepherd, my rock
I'm content to be one of His flock
He's always there to lead me; I know His voice
I'm compelled to follow; I have no choice

I shall never be in want nor want more
As long as Christ is there to go before
I trust the Good Shepherd in all His ways
He will provide for me, forgive me, and amaze

He makes me lie down in pastures green
He quiets my fears, seen and unseen
The presence of the Master fills my soul
I can release all my worries to His control

He leads me beside the waters still and deep
I'm at peace as one of His sheep
He guides me in the Way, the path of right
The lamp at my feet unmistakable and bright

Even in death's shadow, I have no fear
My Lord's comforting presence is always near
His authority is unquestioned; I have to obey
I'm under His protection tomorrow and today

He prepares a grand table just for me
Right there in front of my worst enemy
As His honored guest, I am all aglow
The blessings are so numerous they overflow

Surely, my lot will be goodness and love
Directly from the Heavenly Father above
He will not leave my side, now or ever
And I shall dwell in His house forever.

ATTITUDE OF GRATITUDE

Most Americans have material blessings beyond compare
When we look into our cupboards, they're never bare
When night falls, we never worry about where we'll sleep
Or the safety of our children in a world increasingly bleak

We have more than one car and a garage to park them in
And every couple of years, we buy a new one again
Our savings and checking accounts are never empty
Our closets have shoes, clothes, and jackets aplenty

Our houses are bigger and furnished with every amenity
We send our kids off to college to find their own identity
We can afford insurance for almost every eventuality
And we keep up with most forms of new technology

With all of this affluence, we're just one paycheck from disaster
As a result, we never find the peace and security we're after
We've forgotten that all of our earthly assets are not our own
And they won't matter at all the day the Lord calls us home

Instead of being grateful for the blessings we've been given
Or the fact that, through Christ, our sins have been forgiven
We go through life trying to keep it all under control
And in the process, lose all concern for the health of our soul

People with so much less seem thankful all the more
Wanting in material wealth, in spirit, they're never poor
They're just ever thankful that God sent His only Son
To provide a path to Him when life on Earth is done

So, this Thanksgiving, what shall we do to effect a change?
Can we focus less on the material and our priorities rearrange?
Can we thank Him for our blessings; create a change in attitude?
Isn't it time we go to the Lord and start showing our gratitude?

AUTHOR OF OUR SALVATION

An ambiguous beginning—"It was the best of times and the worst of times"
There's great truth, even today, in Dickens' opening lines
While we work so hard to keep up with technology's frenetic pace
Ethically, morally, and spiritually we're falling from grace

We have every convenience to accomplish more each day
The answers to all of our questions just an iPhone away
That carry-around computer is like a helpful little elf
And we're not far from owning a car that drives itself

But we have lost our day of rest and Sunday gatherings at church
There's no downtime from our online social media search
Like the unhandyman, our socializing is awkward; we're all thumbs
How are we going to respond to each other when the crisis comes?

The online package will soon arrive by drone right at our door
Check-out counters are becoming a thing of the past at our grocery stores
But technological fraud lingers at every corner, just waiting to pounce
Running up charges on our charge cards or draining our accounts

We can communicate with family instantly from anywhere on Earth
And share in the excitement of graduation, wedding, or birth
But we've lost the connections and involvement we had before
Love your neighbor, but do we even know the person next door?

We were in awe when a team of doctors replaced the first human heart
But doctors today routinely replace knees, hips, and most other body parts
We're still the richest nation on Earth, some with incredible wealth
But there are millions of poor who have no access to even basic health

The practice of law, at its best, provides for adjudication of grievances and correction
But today, we are so sensitive and greedy that the law has taken a different direction
Lawyers unapologetically advertise and follow the ambulance wake
Suing doctors who do ground-breaking surgery for even the smallest mistake

Our system of government and way of life is the envy of the world
And yet there are those who refuse to stand when our flag is unfurled
Our free enterprise system has led to an unparalleled standard of living
Yet many game the system, happy to live off those doing the giving

We talk to our computers, they have names, and they talk back
But as far as conversing with each other, we may have lost the knack
The family unit, put together by our Father, is fractured and dispersed
Humanistic answers and attitudes have replaced the God of the Universe

Countries compete at the Olympics as if we're all brothers and friends
But are likely at war psychologically or even militarily at game's end
Technology is supposed to free up our time, make us much less stressed
But we find new ways to burden our time and add to our distress

We're the land of liberty, pursuit of happiness, and free speech
But we shout each other down on our campuses and on our streets
Our schools are supposed to be safe zones for kids to associate and learn
But the disenfranchised bring guns to school when there's nowhere to turn

So, where are we to turn to find the answer, reset our direction?
It's an answer most don't want to hear, this source of correction
Open the Bible, starting on page one, read through to Revelation
God is our only hope, the truth, and the author of our salvation.

BEHIND EVERY SHADOW

These are dark times we're living in
And it can be hard not to just give in
The bad news just seems to get worse every day
And common sense is in complete disarray

COVID doesn't appear to have any end in sight
And peaceful resolution has given way to fight
We're divided like never before in history
Each day brings on a new form of personal misery

Inflation is running rampant on everything we buy
Our leadership regales us with lie after lie
Illegals continue to overrun our Border Patrol
Drugs flooding our country are out of control

Our constitutional republic is falling apart
With leadership that has no soul, no heart
Racism is claimed in almost every police shooting
And becomes the justification for rioting and looting

Our government is becoming a government of the elite
They don't have to follow the same laws we have to meet
Many are hypocrites in the worst sense of what they sanction
Pushing climate control policies while living in multiple mansions

We're living in the shadow of something dark and sinister
We just don't seem to have the antidote to administer
But we all know just a single match can kill the night
And that behind every shadow, there is a light

So, where is this light we crave and anxiously await?
Where is the hope, and how do we open its gate?
It's been there for over 2000 years, knocking on our door
It's Jesus Christ, and we need Him now like never before

He came to Earth as a man to show us how to live
And in dying for our sins, gave all He had to give
I believe there is a Great Awakening coming if we follow Him
And in so doing, shine a light into the shadow of sin.

CABIN IN THE WOODS

Did you ever read the book *Walden* by Henry David Thoreau?
It's a book he writes detailing his thoughts on a variety of themes
All the while living in a rustic cabin and letting modern pleasures go
Experiencing what life could offer when taken to the extremes

I sometimes wonder if all of our conveniences were taken away
No car, no TV, no phone, no groceries at the nearby store
Would we be able to cope, make it through even a single day?
Or would we be looking for a quick exit through the nearest door?

How would we while away our time hour after hour?
What thoughts would come to the surface; what would we write?
Where would we find the motivation, the mental power
To set aside non-essentials and know we'd still be all right?

Could we drop all our stuff and focus only on necessity?
Would the silence be deafening and singing a way to cope
Would loneliness be overwhelming; would we clamor for amenity?
Maybe self-examination would create a path to renewed hope

What new worlds could we explore, what new things to learn
Would our thoughts be so much clearer than ever before?
Would we find new hobbies, become the ultimate bookworm?
And, in doing so, change who we are right to the core

What would our faith look like with all this free time?
Would we read the Bible for the first time from cover to cover?
Would we finally realize Christ needs both our heart and mind?
And might we be more empathic with the struggles of others

I don't know that I would want to respite in a remote cabin
We're social animals, and it's a hard life without interaction
Thoreau spent two years in isolation, no love, no laughin'
Just alone with his thoughts, something I can't even imagine

But then I think there are times when being alone is a plus
Small doses of being alone can help heal our hearts and minds
Time to be quiet and in touch with our Lord, building trust
A time for prayer and building the character that binds

Our society doesn't provide time for this kind of reflection
So the only way is to block out this time each day as we should
We may discover a person we never knew, set a new direction
And love our metaphorical trip to our cabin in the woods.

CHRISTMAS, THE ACRONYM

Did you know that Christmas is an acronym?
With each letter standing for something about Him
It all starts and ends, of course, with the **C**hrist
Who came to Earth to pay the ultimate price

Then comes **H**onor and glory for the Prince of Peace
This we owe to Him at the very least
Next comes **R**esurrection; Death would not win
Christ's appearance restoring life again

Incarnate, taking on flesh this day of His birth
Showing us how we ought to live here on Earth
Sanctification, growing in reliance on the Lord
Marking every day with the study of His Word

We follow on with **T**rust, and with it, faith
In return, we receive both **M**ercy and grace
Mercy we don't deserve and grace that He sends
Directly to us from our Father and Friend

"A" is for **A**lpha and Omega, the beginning and end
Here when it's over; here when it began
"S" is for our **S**avior when we needed Him most
Trinity—Father, Son, and Holy Ghost

So *Christmas* is more than presents under the tree
It's about His presence for you and me
It's a time for us to remember all about Him
And it can be done in a simple acronym.

CONTEMPLATING THE LORD'S PRAYER

Our Father
Not our physical father, but our spiritual one
The one who so loved us He sacrificed His only Son

Who art in Heaven
Heaven is where the God of the Universe resides
But even on Earth, He is always by our side

Hallowed be thy name
His name is above all others since the beginning of time
His name is the one that should fill our hearts and minds

Thy kingdom come
His kingdom will reign, and it will have no end
His enemies will all be vanquished; every knee will bend

Thy will be done on earth as it is in heaven
In heaven and on Earth, God will have His way
And we would do well to follow His will every day

Give us this day our daily bread
Everything we have or will have God provides
Each day is a gift from our Lord Most High

And forgive our trespasses as we forgive those who trespass against us
As God forgives us, we must forgive others
We are all children of God; we're all brothers

And lead us not into temptation
We are in a battle between the spirit and the flesh
Give us discernment and strength to choose best

But deliver us from evil
Protect us from the evil one and his many schemes
His is the easy path, but it's not what it seems

For thine is the kingdom and the power and the glory forever
One day each of us must approach the throne
And acknowledge that He is Lord of all, He alone

Amen
You can believe it
So be it.

CONTRAILS

The other day I noticed several jets moving across the blue
Wending their way, they left a contrail as they flew
The fast-moving planes disappeared before too long
But their contrails lingered awhile before they were gone

It got me to wondering what contrails do we leave?
What stories about us will succeeding generations believe?
Will there be wonderful memories for them to recall?
Or when you're gone, will there be no contrail at all?

Will there be anything for your grandchildren to see?
Or will your story not even qualify as a fading memory?
Will they listen to tales about great-grandpa with glee?
Or will there be just empty pages for your legacy?

There's an old country song I've sung a few times
About leaving this world and what you leave behind
It's not what you take when you leave, you know
It's what you leave behind you when you go

So what are my options; what can I, an old man, really do
There's no paucity of choices, so let me give you a few
Make memories now that your family will never forget
Those contrails with staying power that linger after the jet

Produce a video, organize those photographs, write a book
Do something wild and crazy; an adventure undertook
It's the out-of-character moments, not the blasé
That people will remember long past your day

Set an example for the children to emulate and live by
Show them there's a time for laughter and a time to cry
That challenge brings growth, and the good guy wins
And that regardless of what life brings, you can trust in Him

That truth and integrity will never make the nightly news
But will bring friendships and relationships you'll never lose
And during those times when your life seems in tatters
It's the love of those closest to you that really matters

We have no idea how long we'll have till God reclaims our soul
Because when all is said and done, it's He who's in control
Just remember, when life jets by and your person is out of view
It's your contrail that will determine how they'll remember you.

DISTRACTIONS

Life is full of distractions of all kinds
And they can quickly divert whatever's on our mind
That is especially true of the world we live in today
It is increasingly difficult to keep such diversions at bay

Sometimes I look back at the world of my childhood
Simple, quiet, focused, even boring, but good
We played board games and chatted over a meal
Evening swings on the front porch were a big deal

People dropped by unannounced, and it was okay
The kids were probably out playing ball all day
And we were able to focus on the task at hand
Life felt unhurried, and we listened to the Man

But today, we just seem to be in hurry-up mode
And there is just precious little to lighten our load
It feels like we're in a race, and we're falling behind
Where's the peace we so desperately want to find?

A large part of our frustration comes from technology
Messages bombard us every day on the internet and TV
We can't resist, wherever we are, the call of the iPhone
Downtime is almost non-existent; we're never alone

There's a lot of talk today about ADD or lack of attention span
And there's much about this disorder I don't understand
But I do know the society we live in makes the problem worse
And the distractions all around us are a modern-day curse

So what are we to do to find our own *Golden Pond*?
How do we set all the distractions aside and bond?
How do we begin recovering that sense of family fun?
Actually talking to each other without moving our thumbs

I'm not suggesting we have to give the wonders of technology up
But we have to find ways to step out of this digital rut
We need a time period when we shut all the interruptions down
Talk to each other and to the Lord with no distracting sound

You'll not be able to hear Him above the worldly noise
Make a daily appointment with Him; it's simply a choice.
Make finding your quiet place a part of each and every day
Where it's quiet, and you can hear what the Lord has to say.

HE'S ALIVE

We came from different parts, this disciple band
A common goal in mind—visit the Holy Land
To walk where Jesus walked so long ago
To strengthen our faith and renew our soul

First stop, Caesarea, where Cornelius made news
God's family would not be exclusive to the Jews
The Gentiles would be grafted onto the vine
And have the opportunity for salvation for all time

On to Nazareth, where they rejected their own
How could this carpenter boy be connected to the throne?
He even had the gall to heal the Gentiles and not the Jews
Because they just couldn't accept the Good News

Next up, Mount of Beatitudes, above the sea
Heard the secret to happiness is not fueled by greed
Blessed means God's joy, and it doesn't start
With merit badges and pride, but flows from the heart

A highlight of the trip for sure, baptismal site
Not John, but Max, who performed the rite
Is Jesus the Son of God? The question at hand
Waded into the Jordan and left a new man

Then it's on to Jerusalem, God's holy place
So much history here, times of judgment and grace
From the temple steps, we hear Jesus is ruler of all
And all we have to do is answer the call

We trace the Lord's path from the Olive Mount
Imagining His followers too numerous to count
Laying their cloaks and branches at His feet
Not a horse, but a donkey for the Prince of Peace

We recall Jesus' wrath at the money changers in the temple
And yet still today, merchants set the same example
We visit the Upper Room and the Garden of Gethsemane
Jesus obeying God's plan to save you and me

Via Dolorosa—in English, the way of agony
Aptly describing how Christ suffered for humanity
Carrying that ugly cross up and up to the top of the hill
And nailing our sins to it per His Father's will

The climax of the trip, a visit to the Garden Tomb
Jesus' body would not be confined to this earthen room
The massive rock would move and roll away
And He'd be spiritually and physically alive another day

We had all taken communion hundreds of times
With rituals and services in churches of all kinds
But with the birds chirping in the garden there
And not a dry eye; nothing will ever compare

We were all drawn to this trip in one way or another
This assemblage of Christians, this band of brothers
Death could not hold our Lord in this earthly prison
We know He's alive; we know He's risen.

How God Looks at Prayer

Rick Warren once said if your request is not right, God says "no"
If your timing is not right, God says "slow"
When you are not right, God says "grow"
When all three are right, God says "go"

For years, we've wondered why God answers some prayers
And, at other times, it seems like He's not even there
When our petitions are the most desperate in scope
Is when a non-answer devastates all semblance of hope

But, let's take a look at how God may see things
His ways are not our ways; He's the sovereign King
His understanding surpasses anything we know
Selfish and greedy requests will always get a "no"

God operates in infinity; He has no clock or measured time
So His window of response may not match yours or mine
It's not that He's saying "no," it's more like "not yet"
Testing our patience when our appeal is not expeditiously met

Then there's the issue of us not being in the right place
We may not be spiritually ready to accept His amazing grace
Repair work may be needed before we approach the Lord
We may need to spend time in meditation on His Word

So, you see, there may be reasons for no answer or delay
But that answer could be coming in full measure another day
And when everything is right, God wants you to know
He will answer, and like living water, His blessings will flow

God is not some kind of dispensary or vending machine
His world we don't understand and have never seen
Someday it will all be clear when we approach the throne
And He grants our lifelong request to welcome us home.

I Just Didn't Know

That I would grow up on a dairy farm
As a young man off to college, I would go
That I would have a successful business career
I just didn't know

That I would meet the love of my life
And as husband and wife, together we'd grow
That she'd bring me to You, Lord
I just didn't know

That we'd have two girls who'd make us proud
Exceeding our expectations like a double rainbow
That they would embody all that's good
I just didn't know

That we'd welcome three grandchildren into our world
With feelings of love that would simply overflow
That they'd bring such happiness to our life
I just didn't know

That lifelong Easterners would make the move West
Painting a life as pleasing as a Vincent Van Gogh
And develop new friendships, the lasting kind
I just didn't know

That our retirement would be filled with joy
That we'd travel the country in our rolling chateau
Lifted up by new experiences along the way
I just didn't know

And now, when my life enters the Autumn years
When I look back, it was nothing short of splendid
And it was all under God's control
I just didn't know, but He did.

LOOK FOR THE SHINY IN EVERYTHING

I experienced the negativity of poverty right from the start
And every day since, I fight being a pessimist at heart
In the glass analogy, mine is mostly half empty
Even while prospering, I can see the dark side of plenty

The godly blessings in my life are too numerous to count
And with Him on my side, there's no hurdle I can't surmount
I have every reason to be joyful and expect good
Yet pessimism seems built into my DNA since childhood

I'm always looking for some inspiring words or a catchphrase
To change the way I look at the world and drop this malaise
And the other day, I heard from a friend a line I really like
It was simple and profound—"Look for the shiny things in life"

Isn't that a great encouragement for the world we live in?
Negativity seems to be everywhere, and it's easy to give in
But what if intentional living included looking at the shiny
Finding the happy instead of the sullen and whiny?

We all like shiny things; they just attract our eye
I've thought about this attraction, and I think I know why
They signify something new and different coming our way
A new beginning; the anticipation of a bright new day

We delight in the brand new car, sports car, or sedan
It's a part of shiny we all can relate to and understand
How about the wedding band or engagement ring?
Signifying a shiny new love between queen and her king

But, way more than appearances, shiny is a state of mind
An attitude that enlightens the spirit and frees the mind
If you can see the shiny in every situation, you are blessed
You're a spirit lifter for those who are down and depressed

I know, in my case, I have work to do to find the positive
But I know "looking for the shiny" is the right way to live
It doesn't come about from some kind of self-help book
But rather a commitment to find the good wherever you look

I'm looking to heaven for God to help with my attitude
And I know the "shiny" starts with a large measure of gratitude
After all, what could be shinier than eternity with Him
And filling those spiritual glasses all the way to the brim?

God promised a new Jerusalem, no more pain, no more tears
A brilliant new order, shining with the glory of God always near
Foundations made of jasper, sapphire, and other precious stones
Streets of gold, a gleaming accoutrement for our eternal home

So I think God's promise of a new home like nothing ever seen
Is what attracts us to shiny and provides fuel for our dreams
We know better days are coming to be with our King
Until then, we just need to look for the shiny in everything.

Looking Ahead

Remember when everything was new, and you were just a kid
You just felt like life was moving so excruciatingly slow
You wanted to be a grownup, not Peter Pan, God forbid
Wanting to do what parents do and know what they know

I remember there was a time when I couldn't wait to shave
It may have been only two hairs on my upper lip
Being a man was most important; the thing I craved
And shaving for the first time added credibility to all of it

I had dreams of the great things I would do with my life
A college education, a star athlete, a fancy car for sure
What challenges await, and what my response would be like
Maybe be the one who would conquer cancer, find a cure

The thing I remember most is I was always looking forward
And I was always in a rush to do the next great adult thing
First time driving a car was a major step I looked toward
Like the baby bird, I was forever anxious to take wing

Life went on like that all the way through middle age
Looking forward to whatever would come next
Something exciting was waiting on the succeeding page
How I would handle the changes coming was anyone's guess

Then, as we all do, I moved on to the autumn of my years
And I noticed most of the time I spent looking back
New developments came with a dose of unfounded fears
And I was traveling on an entirely different mental track

My gaze seemed mostly focused on the rearview mirror
Not what was happening right now in front of me
Talking about the good ole days was so much dearer
Relishing my accomplishments and the man I used to be

All my friends seemed to fall into the same backward mode
Memories flowed from our lips like a torrential rain
We lived, backing up, through the stories we told
Reliving the joy, laughter, love, and, yes, the pain

The world was passing us by as we continued looking back
The current world was turning ugly in almost every way
So reminiscing was the only way to keep sanity in the black
Advancements in technology put us further behind every day

Memories are great, but we don't have to live in the past
There are precious moments waiting, still to be lived
New memories can be created by the latter-day enthusiast
If we just embrace the future and what good it has to give

God's plan is always looking forward to better days
The new Jerusalem, the new Garden, and streets of gold
Why should we keep looking back to the old ways?
What's coming should share time with the days of old

The good ole days are not coming back; Jesus is
There's a reason He came to Earth and wound up dead
One day all of Earth will bow down, and the kingdom will be His
It will be a time of joy, and that's why we should look ahead.

MY PRAYER FOR YOU

This is my prayer for you
That you find love in all you do
Comfort on those difficult days
Hugs when things don't go your way

That you have friends to brighten your being
And beauty in everything you're seeing
Confidence when you're in doubt
And rainbows when the rain gives out

Smiles when sadness intrudes
And laughter to change your attitude
Courage to know who you are
And faith to follow the brightest star

Patience when you're in a hurry
Belief that overcomes the worry
Golden sunsets to warm your heart
And turning to God at each day's start.

NORMAL IS NOT RETURNING

I remember my parents talking about the good ole days
Life was simpler; there was a time for rest and the Lord's praise
Rocking on the front porch and watching people go by
Was the climax to a perfect day and the perfect high

Listen to the baby boomers today, and you'll hear a similar refrain
We wish things would turn back to the way they were again
When we didn't need insurance for every possible event
And lawyers weren't chasing ambulances for a payday of 40 percent

When, in class and on the streets, there was respect for authority
The minorities had their say, but rules were established by majority
When hard work and trust in God were the bastions of success
And prayer and fellowship were how we took care of the rest

We knew how a woman was clearly different from a man
Only two sexes, created according to God's Master Plan
We respected history and learned from it, whether good or bad
Eliminating the parts we didn't like was not a choice we had

We grew up knowing we had a large part to play in our fate
We relied on family if necessary, not the welfare state
Never thought of taking a knee for the flag of the country we adore
While our soldiers fight for our freedom on some distant shore

In our time, the highest of the high came from a bottle of beer
The hard drugs were available, but we knew to stand clear
Spending we thought required money in your account
But our government put that restriction completely in doubt

And so, we look longingly for the day when things will again be norm
When the upside-down world we're in returns to a saner form
When "love thy neighbor" is more than just a thought
And right here on Earth, we'll live and love as God taught

If that actually happens, I will be the first to stand and applaud
But I think the only answer to this mess is in the hands of God
One day, the trumpet will sound, and all control will be His
Normal is not returning; Jesus is.

PENNIES IN THE PARKING LOT

Many times you've probably walked across a parking lot
And noticed a penny on the ground, likely as not
Did you take a moment to bend down and retrieve it?
Or did you just think it's not worth the effort and leave it?

In my case, I know I've often just left it on the ground
In too big a hurry to even think about bending down
After all, it won't buy anything; it's mostly worthless
An annoyance that should be taken out of service

But if you look a little closer, the penny has a lot to say
On it, a great president, Lincoln, is prominently displayed
On the left side, you'll see the crux of our founding, "liberty"
And above Lincoln, "In God We Trust" for all to see

On the back side, you'll see "United States of America"
It's like a reminder of unity past, a different era
"E Pluribus Unum" reminds us of how we were once together
One unified voice that made us stronger; made us better

So you see, that worthless penny contains quite a bit of history
And why we treat it with such disrespect is something of a mystery
It represents many of the values we Americans hold dear
A reminder of a time when our principles were crystal clear

The population of the United States is about 323 million souls
All accounted for by headcount in the latest census polls
What if each of us picked up one penny a year in the parking lot
And dumped all those pennies into one big charity pot

By my calculation, that would be 3.2 million dollars—plenty
To justify each of us stopping on our way to pick up that penny
Think of all the good that could be done for those in need
And at no cost to us, such a simple kindness indeed

Sometimes I wonder if God Himself throws those pennies there
Just to test our sense of humility and the brotherhood we share
Maybe our life has become too haughty, or maybe we just forgot
The intrinsic value of the pennies in the parking lot.

POETRY CONNECTS US TO LIFE

I write poetry as a hobby; from it, I derive great pleasure
The ones that strike at the heart are a real treasure
Life has a rhythm to it, a balance, and so does a poem
It's confirmation of shared feelings; that we're not alone

When a poem has a point germane to the real-life foray
It connects to people, what they do and what they say
Something they never considered may be driven home
By the skilled words of a poet, recorded in his latest poem

Like a kind word, a poem comes straight from the heart
It may not turn around every attitude, but it's a start
Life is full of troubles, and we long to escape from reality
And for just a while, the poem can be a welcome fantasy

Life is full of troubles, pathos, correction, and fear
A good poem can bring hope to an otherwise dismal year
Let's not forget that a poem is a precursor to every song
A timeless blend of words and music can never be wrong

A heartfelt message to a friend in time of need
Part of a recovery process, or at least the seed
There's just something catchy about words that rhyme
That may stick in your head for the rest of your time

Believer or not, poems often have a spiritual element
Words that are inspiring, creative, and eloquent
Lines that may hit you exactly where you're walking
And cut right through all that bravado you're talking

Life can take us from the highest mountain to the lowest floor
And we can understand it all through a poetic metaphor
Life is lived one day at a time, easy street or cutting like a knife
But whatever it is, you can be sure the poetry will connect us to life.

RESURRECTING AMERICA

One of Webster's definitions of resurrection is a resurgence or revival
We all know about "The Resurrection" that portends eternal survival
And there's been nothing since to remotely compare to that event
But several times in our history, we've come together as if heaven sent

Our forefathers structured our country on Christian principles
But we've drifted away to such an extent they're barely visible
We disdain prayer and have taken God out of public places
We've lost concern for each other, and it's written on our faces

We fight and bicker, even resort to calling each other names
There's class warfare even though our life goals are largely the same
Instead of "us" in our dialogue, there's likely a lot more "me"
And as years go by, there seem to be more ways we disagree

But every once in a while, the Lord uses circumstances to call us back
When the problem can't be fixed with psychology, consultation, or Prozac
And people finally admit the trouble is beyond what they can handle
When they've considered all other alternatives, explored every other angle

Situations that come to mind are world wars and the Great Depression
Times when everyone had to sacrifice, and everything was in question
The 9/11 attack is a more recent example of catastrophe at our door
In each of these times, we came together as Americans like never before

E Pluribus Unum was more than just a slogan; many became one
We were united in our attitudes and worked together till victory was won
With perfect strangers, we extended our help to show we cared
And even the doubters could be heard talking to the Lord in prayer

In short, it was a resurrection of when this country was a band of brothers
When we put aside our personal ambitions in order to help others
And when we do this, it is proven we are a force to be reckoned with
That the American response to a crisis is more than just a myth

Our latest challenge is the coronavirus, and we will overcome it as well
Just how that story will play out and how we change, no one can tell
But neighbors are helping neighbors, and families are reconnecting
Governments and corporations are part of the American spirit resurrecting

Heroes are everywhere, serving in our hospitals and in their homes
Reaching out to others who cannot get out and are suffering alone
States better off are sending their ventilators to other states
And everywhere we look, concern for others has replaced hate

So when this crisis is over, and things return to normal once more
Will we have learned anything about how to treat those next door?
Will we have made necessary changes to keep ourselves protected?
Will we return to the Lord in prayer and truly become resurrected?

Or will we revert back to the ugliness evident in recent years?
I pray we give it all to the Lord to trust in Him and calm our fears
That we acknowledge again our forefathers so long ago had it right
That everything starts with God, His love, His power, and His might.

SANITIZING EVERYTHING

COVID-19 has changed our world and not for the better
It seems to have taken away the joy of being together
We're always on alert that all are obeying what's asked
Are we six feet apart, and why aren't you wearing a mask?

Wherever we go, we reach for the sanitizer jar
Disinfecting door handles, chairs, and even our cars
We hide in our bubbles, also known as our homes
Seeking some security at the expense of being alone

I'm not saying we shouldn't take COVID as a serious concern
But I wonder, with all of our knowledge, what have we learned?
Do we know nothing about how the body builds immunity?
How it's our best defense and fights disease beautifully?

It just seems we've all retreated to the safety of our bubble
Believing if we're never exposed, we'll stay out of trouble
But that doesn't give our body mechanisms a chance to work
To build up natural antibodies to all the contagions that lurk

Remember back when we were kids, sometimes eating dirt
And how drinking out of the hose never caused any real hurt
A peanut allergy was something we never even heard of
A peanut butter sandwich was proof of a mother's love

Our bodies are teeming with microscopic organisms, aka germs
And, in protecting our health, they each take their turn
Maybe that's why the five-second rule for food on the floor
Became the acceptable standard this situation called for

We have a lot of knowledge, but we aren't at all wise
We've allowed our world to become super-sanitized
And this applies not only to our health but our relationships
Being ultra-careful, we don't offend with one of our quips

We take everything so seriously; there's no room for a joke
For fear of what push-back or hostility it might provoke
The result is we spend more time with those who think as we do
And divisiveness and tunnel vision go deeper than we want them to

In Judeo-Christian circles, forgiveness and kindness are virtues
But today, we're so sensitive the simplest affront makes the news
Our nation, once the envy of the world, has become a nation of tribes
Sexual, political, and racial divisions dominate our lives

We even want to sanitize our history; make changes to the past
But whitewashing dark moments teaches us nothing that will last
Pulling down historical monuments in lawless celebration
Is just an attempt to remove the stories that helped shape this nation

There seems to be no clear path to end this kind of discord
And I don't think that will change until we return to our Lord
Only then will we find that it's to the human race we all belong
We don't need to sanitize; just harmonize to the same song

Only then will we show each other an appropriate respect
And not worry whether everything we say is politically correct
This sounds like a kind of unachievable nirvana, I realize
But it can happen if we take a step back and don't over-sanitize

I don't know what God's plan is. One day, I hope to understand
But I'm pretty sure this was not what He intended for man
Sickness and tribal warfare is all we're ever going to bring
If we think the answer is just sanitizing everything.

SOMETHING MORE

There's more to living than just surviving
More to success than just arriving
More to spirituality than just believing
And more to happiness than just achieving

There's more to satisfaction than just status and cash
More ways to profit than greed unabashed
More to music than just the dance
And more to a marriage than just romance

There's more to sport than the winning goal
More to relationships than who's in control
More to courtesy than opening a door
And more to growth than just wanting more

There's more to golf than just breaking par
More ways to demonstrate just who you are
More to helping the poor and those in need
Than just the checkbook to help them succeed

There's more to education than just a degree
More to faith than what you can see
More to believing than the mind and the intellectual
And more to God's Word than just conceptual

There's more to prayer than elegant words
It's what's on your heart that God prefers
There's more to talking with God than endless requests
Applauding His mercy and grace pleases Him best

Jesus said His reason for coming to Earth
Was to have life and to have it for all it was worth
He returned to the Father to show us the way
Until we join Him, we're to live to the fullest each day

There are deeper levels to reach in just about every situation
And I think it all started with the beginning—creation
Just as the Universe presents endless new adventures to explore
So, in life, there's always that element of something more.

SUNDAY IS COMING

There are many religions that all stand by what they believe
They may even claim all other religions are being deceived
But Christians hold one thing that's different from all the rest
That Christ arose from the grave, achieving victory over death

Satan probably crowed when Jesus suffered and died on the cross
But God in heaven had too great a plan for all to be lost
And while what happened on Friday was ugly and stunning
Final victory would be His because Sunday was coming

Our world today can also be ugly and in much the same way
Lies, fraud, and cheating are still part of each day
It can be depressing and hard to follow Jesus, the King
When crime and deception infiltrate everything

We're not beaten and crucified like Jesus, not even close
Our suffering is more emotional, fearing rejection the most
But when we feel like giving up and finally succumbing
Our strength comes from knowing that Sunday is coming

The biblical principles Jesus taught us while here on Earth
Are being questioned at every turn as to their worth
We're doing our best, Lord, to carry the torch, keep on becoming
Knowing that Friday will pass and Sunday is coming

We believe we will follow Jesus one day and live again
Because He made a path for us to join Him despite our sin
That even with all the corruption, distortion, and cunning
We can be optimistic and resilient because Sunday is coming

So when someone puts you down, keep your eyes on the prize
Because one day, as Jesus promised, you too will rise
To your Master's outstretched arms, you'll soon be running
Because all your Fridays will be over and Sunday is coming.

THE PERFECT PLAN

Did you ever wonder what life might have been?
What would it be like if you could somehow start again?
What if your situation was totally different at birth?
Would you contribute more or less to Planet Earth?

I was born into poverty, but what if I was rich?
Would I be altruistic or just worship the money itch?
I was a country boy, but what if I was a city slicker?
Would I have climbed the corporate ladder quicker?

What if I was smarter, not just an average Joe?
What if I was educated at Harvard, not Buffalo?
What if I could have danced like Fred Astaire?
What if I had the means of a multi-millionaire?

But, on the other hand, what if I was born in another land?
Inhospitable places like Syria, Iraq, or Iran?
Places where a dictator's authority reigns supreme
Where the liberties I enjoy are just a dream

What if I had no home, just living on the street?
Every day a challenge for food and shoes on my feet
Sickness and exposure to cold a constant threat
Begging on the roadways for whatever I could get

Yes, the life I've lived could have been so much different
The things accomplished so much more or less significant
But when I look back, there's one thing I understand
There are no coincidences; it was God who dealt this hand

I'm right where God wanted me, what He ordained
And without Him, I know my life would not be the same
So instead of being wistful about what might have been
I'm just so thankful that, for me, God had the perfect plan.

WE'RE ALL HYPOCRITES

Someone who professes one thing and yet does the opposite
That's pretty much the definition of a hypocrite
In our world, they are prevalent at all levels of society
Often the one I claim to be far exceeds the real me

We profess that telling the truth is always wise
But spin, exaggerations, and half-truths still qualify as lies
We profess that the love for our spouse is forever strong
But don't see lustful glances as anything wrong

We profess that greed is not one of our faults or sins
But our lifestyle tells a different story time and again
We profess humility, but accomplishments puff up our pride
We profess to be Christian, but did we really change inside?

We profess to be happy for our neighbor's success
But secretly covet his material possessions, if we have less
We claim to drink only in moderation and to be sociable
But at the party, our alcohol consumption is negotiable

We profess not to ever use God's name in vain
But it's still a bad habit we can't completely contain
And while we don't condone movies using the F-word
If the movie is otherwise good, we'll watch it undeterred

Non-Christians complain about Christians "holier than thou"
We should never pretend to be perfect; we don't know how
The Bible says there is no one who does good—not even one
That our only hope is salvation through God's only Son

Paul, the Apostle, said, "I do what I don't want to do"
And for all of us, isn't that statement oh so true?
We hide it all under the various masks we wear
The real "us" is never completely laid bare

So what are we to do? Are we just hopeless in our sin?
Isn't seeking forgiveness a good place to begin?
Is there a point where we no longer qualify for it?
And so we just go on with our life as a hypocrite?

Jesus addressed this when Peter asked how many times
Are we to forgive someone who steps out of line?
Remember Jesus' answer—seventy times seven
That is, there's no limit on the path to heaven

So there's no question we should be doing our best every day
To make sure we're following Jesus' teaching of the Way
But if Paul couldn't live up to Jesus' behavioral plan
What would make you think there's a chance we can?

Let's let God be our judge at our heavenly trial
But treat each transgression with prayer all the while
And when we're with others, freely admit
We're not perfect; we need forgiveness like any hypocrite.

SURRENDER—HUMILITY

"Come to me, all you who are weary and burdened, and I will give you rest"
(Matthew 11:28, NIV).

"Humble yourselves before the Lord, and he will lift you up"
(James 4:10, NIV).

ARE YOU SWIMMING UPSTREAM?

Why does it seem we all like to swim upstream?
What's the allure; what's the goal, the dream?
There must be something more than a childish wish
To make us follow the example of a salmon fish

There's not only the power of the raging water to overcome
There are barriers to jump over and even death to some
What prevents us from giving in and just letting go?
Why can't we just lay back and go with the flow?

I think all this effort comes from a kind of macho role
Leave it all up to us; we need to be in control
I'll just keep on stroking, no matter the outcome
I'll only look for help when there's nowhere to run

But watch what happens if we admit it's not up to us
Life is so much easier if we just step off the struggle bus
God said, know that I am God and be still
I'm God, and you're not; stop fighting My will

I have plans for your life, plans that will prosper you
Haven't I already shown you how much I love you?
Release your grip, and I'll take you through the wake
To where the water glasses out to a peaceful lake

When you finally admit that it's Me in control
When you acknowledge that I touch your very soul
When you freely accept Me and your burdens release
Then you will know what it feels like on that lake of peace

You were never meant to be a salmon, splashing about
Before you exhaust yourself and completely burn out
Reach out to Me, and we'll walk this walk together
And you'll know this life of yours can be so much better.

AT THE DOORSTEP

At the doorstep, agonizingly short on earthly years
Looking at a life woefully short of the mark
Hoping Your promises will overcome my fears
That the ramp will be lowered to Your spiritual ark

I know nothing of the crossing ahead of me
I pray the evil one awaits not on the other side
All I have to offer is a life of sin and inconsistency
Your love traded for an inflated sense of pride

I'm completely at Your mercy, a lost sheep
There's nothing at all I can do to secure my place
My sins are plentiful, embarrassing, and deep
I'm totally reliant on Your forgiveness and grace

I envision myself coming weakly before Your throne
Falling on my knees, too embarrassed to raise my head
I look for support, but this is a trip I must make alone
I deserve eternity in hell, but I yearn for heaven instead

I know I should have focused less on the things of Earth
And as You watched, I know You must have wept
I am naked; nothing do I bring forward of any worth
My days are numbered, and I stand at the doorstep

The hours grow shorter with each passing day
Each day I approach closer to the Great Unknown
All that's left now is to accept Your judgment and pray
That when that time comes, You'll welcome me home.

HIS WAY

We've all listened to and sung the words to Frank Sinatra's "My Way"
I believe we covet the idea of being in charge of everything
Deep down in our human emotions, don't we all just want to say
I did it my way and chime in with our voices when Frank sings?

Its basic message is, despite many mistakes, I have no regrets
When things got rough, I faced it on my own and stood tall
Despite the odds stacked against me, I took on all threats
I had my losses, but I overcame every challenge; as I recall

As you listen to the words, there is not an ounce of humility
Rather it is filled with self-aggrandizement and pride
And, as we look around today, it's what's going on in society
Accomplishments are placed high on a hill and amplified

Now don't get me wrong I have sung this song a thousand times
And the words and tune resonate somewhere deep in my soul
It's addictive as it seems to take over my heart and mind
And leads me to believe that I have it all under my control

The song ends with say what you feel and never kneel
The record shows I took the blows and did it my way
But isn't it God we rely on to help us through our ordeals?
And aren't the blows softer when we're on our knees to pray?

I have spent more than half my life trying to do it my way
There were many trials and tribulations along that road
In those few moments when I was quiet, I could hear God say
Come closer to Me; I will give you peace and lighten your load

Free will battles God's will, and humility has become a lost ideal
We are not obedient to our Creator when He touches our ear
We don't think that voice we hear with our heart is real
We just can't leave behind the "me syndrome" we revere

After many years of walking a misguided path all alone
I've learned to try to turn it all over to Him each and every day
And I know on that last day on Earth when He calls me home
I will be forever grateful that He showed me "His Way."

I Woke up This Morning, and I'm Not Dead

What shall I do with this day that lies before
What adventure awaits as I walk out the door
I hope I'm ready for whatever lies ahead
Because I woke up this morning, and I'm not dead

Will I meet someone I've never met before
Or will it be an old friend from way back yore
I hope I'll learn something new, as it's been said
Because I woke up this morning, and I'm not dead

Will it be some kind of calamity that's in store
Or some kind of victory causing my spirit to soar
Maybe I'll delve into a book that I've never read
Because I woke up this morning, and I'm not dead

Will I be a blessing to someone who needs my help
Bringing satisfaction like I've never felt
I hope I don't just lie there, lounging in bed
Because I woke up this morning, and I'm not dead

Will it be time with family—fun and so well spent
Will it start with a quiet prayer heaven sent
The opportunities are limitless, a to zed
Because I woke up this morning, and I'm not dead

I know God is there and will direct my path
I pray that He showers me with love, not His wrath
If I but listen to His calling, I know I'll be led
Because I woke up this morning, and I'm not dead

Maybe the day will be routine, nothing new coming my way
In any case, I still expect it to be a wonderful day
I plan to take it one day at a time, not look ahead
Because I woke up this morning, and I'm not dead

Will the world be a better place when this day is done
Will I bring into someone's dreary life a little fun
I hope my focus is not on me but on others instead
Because I woke up this morning, and I'm not dead

I'm waiting on You, Lord; what's Your plan
My life today is completely in Your hands
Father, give me this day, my daily bread
Because I woke up this morning, and I'm not dead.

JESUS WEPT

It's the shortest verse in the Bible, John 11:35
It had been four days since Lazarus was last seen alive
Some have said it was with empathy that Jesus grieved
Others that it was sorrow because they didn't believe

When push came to shove, they did not believe He was King
That He had control of all creation and every happening
That He had the power to make all things new
And that there was absolutely nothing He couldn't do

I wonder if Jesus looks down on us now and the way we live
And weeps with how divisive we've become and reticent to forgive
How we shade the truth, comfortable with distortion and lies
How we so easily turn away from Him in our daily lives

That Jesus was 100 percent God and 100 percent man Christians accept
And He showed both dimensions of His nature when He wept
He is not some remote God who cares little for what we do
His passion just shows how much He loves both me and you

I'm sure He weeps when He sees what's happened to our country
How we fight with each other and disrespect all authority
How we've lost our moral compass and the breakdown of family
And no longer see reading and studying His Word as a necessity

On the other hand, He is jubilant when He sees our sacrifice
Helping others and using our gifts to bring them to Christ
Sharing our testimony of who we were and how we came to believe
Becoming that trusted friend who, through it all, will never leave

I think there's a reason "Jesus wept" is the shortest verse in the Bible
His tears dry quickly when He sees us following Him as a disciple
Humbly turning it all over to Him, that's what He and the Father expect
And His joy in seeing that overcomes any recollection of "Jesus wept."

SIMMER IN PRAYER

Solar tea is made with water and tea caressed by the sun
Its essence is released as a gentle, unhurried process is run
You cannot brew a proper tea with a satisfying taste
Using extremely hot water and tea made in haste

Likewise, my Master is at work, and I'm simmering as His tea
He has many different ways to bring out the essence of me
It's a slow process as He teaches me the wonders of Him
Removing the bitter taste that comes with the intrusion of sin

Sometimes I try to take over the process, brew my own me
The result of this free will is expected and easy to foresee
This brew, when finished, is rancid; not at all drinkable
And going my own way, completely unthinkable

I am steeped in His love, and slowly I'm beginning to see
That He has just the right process for the flavor of me
And all I have to do to make me a brew beyond compare
Is to go to the Lord in worship and simmer in prayer.

SPIRITUAL WINDOW

1955
I was ten years old
My "spiritual window" was dark and cold
My parents didn't know Christ, and neither did I
That Jesus was just a man I didn't see as a lie

1965
I was twenty years old
My "spiritual window" was opaque; nothing to behold
I was told Jesus was my Savior and Lord
But it didn't matter because I hadn't read His Word

1975
I was thirty years old
Jesus was the key to my "spiritual window," I was told
I was an arrogant and stubborn atheist
Didn't try to believe even when my life was a mess

1985
I was forty years old
My "spiritual window" was foggy as I took off the blindfold
Baptized and accepted Jesus as my Savior
The problem was it didn't drastically change my behavior

1995
I was fifty years old
My "spiritual window" showed me Jesus was gaining a foothold
I still thought when push came to shove, it was up to me
Turning my life over to Jesus, I just could not see

2005
I was sixty years old
My "spiritual window" had lost its fog, and Jesus had won my soul
He sent a friend who brought me into a lifelong relationship
I finally understood living water and took a big sip

2015
Now I'm seventy years old
That "spiritual window" is crystal clear and trimmed in gold
Sometimes as I write, His spirit has me on a different page
And I know now that everything with Him gets clearer with age.

THE STUPID YEARS

Thank You, Lord, for getting me through the "Stupid Years"
When You could not compete with the influence of my peers
Those years when I was absolutely certain I knew it all
I had a conscience, but it was mostly muted, as I recall

Mom would give me instructions not to do this or that
Whatever was taboo was the thing I couldn't wait to get at
I made fun of other kids who were different from me
The harm that I brought on them, I just could not see

I drove recklessly, not even considering the speed limit
After all, I'd be late for some party if I didn't put a kick in it
The girls were the object of more than just casual glances
And I'm thankful they resisted my less-than-innocent advances

I went to church, but I was just playing a bit part
The message hit the brain but missed the heart
The mask I wore covered almost all of my ineptitude
Back then, I believed that somehow I fooled even You

When my life should have been busy chasing after Thee
Instead, I was chasing advancement up the money tree
Trying desperately to keep up with the other boys
Accumulating a bigger bank account and adult toys

There were times, Lord, when I took Your name in vain
I know my actions probably made You groan in pain
I didn't know the Ten Commandments were in Your hand
And the death and resurrection I didn't care to understand

What's amazing to me is how You let me go on this way
Knowing that You could turn me around someday
That, one day, I would come to my senses and realize
That each life has meaning when seen through Your eyes

You would not let me be a victim of my own stupidity
Instead, You fostered a life of purpose and humility
I've heard it said, "You can't fix stupid," but it's untrue
All we ever have to do is just turn it all over to You

I am so thankful, Lord, that You stuck with me through it all
That in later years I heard Your voice and answered Your call
That I can now look to You for forgiveness, not dread
And know for certain the truth of every word You ever said

I believe, Lord, that many youths are much like me today
Thank You for working with them to change their ways
Even though they think they're in control and just don't hear
I ask that You protect them, Lord, through the "Stupid Years."

THIS IS MY PRAYER

I'm a sinner, Lord, but I want to be free
I'm prideful; help me live in humility
Illuminate my darkness with Your redeeming light
Give me the wisdom to separate wrong from right

Bring love front and center, Lord, instead of hate
Bring forth the kindness that should not wait
Give me some of the patience of Job
Help me spread the seed You want sowed

Help me be truthful, dispensing with the lie
Make me unafraid of the day I die
To turn away from the love of money and greed
Not coveting the things that I don't need

Help me be a witness to the circle of influence I'm in
First and foremost, let them see me as a friend
Help me be joyful in all times, good and bad
Encouraging others when times are sad

Strengthen me, Lord, in my weakness
I'm nothing without Your forgiveness
Help me find, Lord, my fruitful place
And shower me with Your amazing grace

Help me, Lord, be the Christian You want me to be
So that those around me know I follow Thee
Give me the words, Lord, that I need in prayer
I know You're listening in the great somewhere

Protect my family, Lord, keeping them safe and secure
And bring them closer to You with hearts that are pure
These are my entreaties to You, Lord and King
I know for certain You can handle everything

Make me, Lord, the kind of man who can be
With You and the angels through all eternity
I have no accomplishments on which I can stand
I'm totally reliant on your merciful hand

This is my prayer, Lord, on this day
That You would direct my steps toward Your way
That You would help me be the man You created me to be
That I would be welcomed at the gates of eternity.

Whose Feet Will You Wash Today?

Why do we have such a struggle with pride versus humility?
Why do we equate passing credit to others with a loss of dignity?
Is pride part of our sinful nature, somehow built into our DNA?
Or do we learn it, episode by episode—piecemeal, day by day?

Maybe it's some of each, but I know it starts at an early age
Who can run the fastest, throw the ball the farthest, upstage
We want our achievements rewarded with higher marks and praise
Taking our rightful place on the podium, basking in those glorious rays

We instill in our children the importance of confidence
But, at what point does confidence cross over to arrogance?
When does the home run trot turn into obnoxious swagger?
When playing together as a team is all that should matter

Being competitive is not wrong until it becomes all about me
And the flames of pride are fanned every day by society
World-class athletes claiming they're the greatest of all time
And politicians taking credit for accomplishments of every kind

We are taught that we can make it happen; it's within our control
Step up to the plate; you don't need anyone, just set your goal
And when we achieve, we naturally take the credit we believe is our due
Even though it was the contribution of others that brought us through

The TV commercials belt out extravagant claims night and day
But when we try their products, they either don't work, or they're just okay
Every claim seems to come with a strong measure of hyperbole
And it's not tempered at all by even a hint of humility

We're quick to take credit for any kind of accomplishment or success
And just as quick to distance ourselves from association with the rest
We don't even think of what drives us this way or question why
It just seems natural to start each sentence with the pronoun "I"

And yet we have wonderful examples of humility right at hand
Consider the greatest modern-day pastor, evangelist Billy Graham
He says he has nothing to offer thousands when he begins to preach
And without the power of the Holy Spirit that he'd have nothing to teach

Then there's the apostle Paul, probably the greatest disciple of all time
Time after time, in deference to Christ, he put his life on the line
Advising his followers to value others above self
Putting their own interests on hold to offer others help

The most astounding example of humility to ever be found
Is at the Last Supper with the Apostles gathered round
When the most famous meal had begun but was not yet complete
The God of the Universe lowered Himself to wash His disciples' feet

Humility may not be as difficult, after all, as it would seem to be
Perhaps we can make a start by beginning our sentences with "we"
Soon we'll see that using this technique is not only better but preferred
And that despite what our culture teaches, humility is not a dirty word.

It will not be an easy thing to do solely through the efforts of self
It will take the power of the Holy Spirit to put pride on the shelf
So take the next step to prevent pride from having its way
Metaphorically speaking, whose feet will you wash today?

GRACE—SALVATION

"For it is by grace you have been saved, through faith—and this is not from yourselves, it is the gift of God" (Ephesians 2:8, NIV).

"For the grace of God has appeared that offers salvation to all people" (Titus 2:11, NIV).

EGR

Someone cuts you off on the interstate
Or blows their horn because they just can't wait
Or gives you the high sign from their car
You don't react because you know about EGR

Someone cuts in front of you in the ticket line
You'd really like to give them a piece of your mind
But you hold back, not choosing the verbal spar
You recognize they're just someone in need of EGR

You meet someone who regales about his multiple degrees
And how this knowledge helped him become a corporate VP
The implication being you fell short in not getting that far
Time to tone down your feelings and bring out the EGR

There's the one who likes to dominate every conversation
On any subject, he can pontificate without cessation
In every gathering, he's the unquestionable star
And in need of a large helping of EGR

There's the guy at the party with no social graces
Saying all the wrong things in all the wrong places
May have made too many trips to the wine bar
Loud and obnoxious, he needs mega-doses of EGR

We all know those who, if put in charge, could do it better
But we know them as just commentators, not go-getters
Not the kind to roll up their sleeves; that's not who they are
But we're obligated to show them love through EGR

Four of us go out to dinner, but when the check comes around
Those friends with alligator arms just can't be found
They're not French, but they've gone "*au revoir*"
We dish out not only the money but the EGR

Some just go through life high on the "grumpy scale"
They see the negative side of everything without fail
I have to admit I'm one who often sees the half-empty jar
I'm so glad my wife and friends offer plenty of EGR

We encounter EGR people every day in our travels
At times, our patience comes nearly unraveled
But then, the Lord speaks, and we are inspired
To give a pass to those of Extra Grace Required.

FOOTPRINTS ON MY HEART

Almost everyone knows the "Footprints in the Sand" poem
Showing us that in troubled times we are not alone
That we can handle it all when things are stable
But He carries us when we're weak and unable

There are two sets of footprints when times are fun
But when trouble develops, there seems to be only one
This is a great analogy that I wouldn't want to dismiss
But I think there's at least one other way to look at this

Most of the time, I noticed there were two sets of prints
God and I walking together; that made sense
But occasionally, there was only one set of tracks evident
Times when I no longer wanted or needed His consent

My tracks wandered off and were quickly washed away
But God's were there waiting for me to return to His way
And when I did, He completely forgave my excursion
Took my hand again, and we walked off my every burden

You would think I'd have learned my lesson, but I wander still
It's a gift that God gave all of us, and it's called free will
He wants us to walk with Him, but it's still our choice
He speaks quietly, and we must listen intently to hear His voice

One day I hope our footprints will run for miles side by side
That we will always walk together and I'll have nothing to hide
That every day of my life, God and I will never be apart
And His footprints will not only be in the sand but on my heart.

FOOTSTEPS OF DORIAN GRAY

You may recall the book *A Picture of Dorian Gray*
Oscar Wilde created quite a stir with it in his day
It's about a handsome young man who's all the rage
Despite his advancing years, he just never seems to age

But a painting of him at home tells quite a different tale
The painting picks up all the signs of aging in great detail
Every act of debauchery is recorded right there on his face
While the mask he wears in real life conceals his disgrace

For every sin he commits, the painting develops new wrinkles
New signs of aging appear—scars, moles, and pimples
The painting becomes decrepit—bald and tired, with sagging skin
While Dorian keeps his childish good looks and winsome grin

John Wooden once said, "Reputation is what people think you are"
And on that alone, some may elevate you to the class of superstar
But he defined character as what you really are, as seen by God
You could present a great face to the world, and it be just a facade

Of course, none of us have a painting in the attic like Dorian Gray
But God has such a painting that makes Him sad every day
He wants so much for our painting and our real self to be the same
A heart that's pure, a mind that's clean, and a soul absent of shame

He knew that, on our own, we could never be reconciled to Him
That only by sending His Son could death be brought to sin
So that when Christ intercedes for us on Judgment Day
Our painting and our real self will the same picture display

So, I pray you're not a double agent in the way you lead your life
That who you are in public and when no one's watching are just alike
That you're becoming more like Christ each and every day
And not following in the misguided footsteps of Dorian Gray.

God Doesn't Grade on a Curve

It all starts when we're very young
Comparing ourselves to others in what we've done
Our good is better than someone else's good
And our bad is not as bad, just misunderstood

The professor gives us a grade on a college exam of 22
We realize in horror it's an "F;" nothing we can do
We anguish, but then mercifully, he posts the curve
We're elevated to a "B," completely undeserved

Likewise, it follows on in our business career
We sweat it out with the layoff announcement near
But the manager has ranked us from one to ten
And by the grace of his "curve," we're safe once again

And so it goes in every facet of life on Earth
We don't receive the grade that reflects our worth
With the bear chasing, we don't have to have the fleetest of feet
It's only the slowest of foot that we have to beat

But when it comes to who goes to heaven, it's a different game
It won't matter if we're better, worse, or just the same
We'll stand before the Father and our record He'll observe
Normal probability won't matter; there are no points in reserve

God's standard is perfection, nothing short of 100 percent
And on our own, there's no chance of that standard being met
It's only through Jesus Christ we get the grade we don't deserve
He's the only way because God doesn't grade on a curve.

GOD'S ALWAYS THERE

The other night I decided to lounge in my enticing spa
Sampling God's living water below His starry cup
Knowing that I would be mesmerized and in awe
If I just set my mind at ease, laid back, and looked up

It had been a long day with tribulation everywhere
Where was my God during this very trying day?
On a day like this, I wondered, does He even care?
Can I draw inspiration from the heavens when I pray?

I can't tell you the disappointment with what I saw
The clouds of worry and doubt took over my mind
They blocked out the stars as if He wasn't there at all
And without His light, all positivity lagged behind

I turned my focus to the worldly things all around
I couldn't get my mind off them, hard as I might try
I was stuck on all those things I know just bring me down
And questioned God right there as I peeked again at the sky

What a beautiful shock it was as I garnered a second glance
The clouds erased, and in their place, a starry, starry sea
They were all there twinkling as if in some heavenly dance
And it reminded me God is there even when I cannot see

So when you have days that are troubling and God seems absent
Look to the heavens, beyond the clouds, and breathe deeply the air
You'll just wonder where all your worldly concerns went
And you'll realize that, behind the clouds, God's always there.

GOD'S "HAIL MARY" LOVE

Whether it's pro or college, Americans are football nuts
Sitting on the edge of their seats with every hut, hut, hut
Whether it's an interception, fumble, or 50-yard bomb
We just can't get enough of the passion trip we're on

The game comes with terminology all its own, unique
The blitz, the sack, the scramble, and the fly sweep
The quarterback calls an audible if the play's not right
Hoping for the perfect call and a run to daylight

Of course, the end of the game entails the two-minute warning
A time when senses are heightened and passions burning
When all hope is lost as to how to defeat your adversary
There's a final toss into the end zone called the "Hail Mary"

Referred to as the "Hail Mary Pass" because it comes with prayer
Out of options, they're leaving it up to the Man upstairs
It's a jump ball in the end zone because it's all that's left
And who comes down with the ball is anyone's guess

But do you know that God had a "Hail Mary Option" as well?
It was His last ditch effort to save us from the terror of hell
The Old Testament documents 4000 years of pain and grace
Trying to bring His people to Him in that intimate place

There was the beginning in Eden with God and man together
Nothing since has been as beautiful, and no relationship better
But Adam and Eve messed it up and were banned from the garden
And ever since, it's been alternately love and hearts hardened

It was so bad that God flooded the world but never gave up heart
Rather extending His love to Noah and his family for a new start
He chose Abram to bring forth descendants too numerous to count
But the Israelites rejected Him and became slaves down and out

God delivers them from the bondage of Egypt and splits the Red Sea
But mostly, they complain that things are not what they should be
God sends prophet after prophet to encourage them to repent
But they reject everyone, even killing some He sent

Nebuchadnezzar vanquishes Jerusalem because of their guilt
The Israelites turn back to God, and the temple is rebuilt
But it's not long before they wander again and again
Each time asking for forgiveness but turning back to sin

Aren't we a lot like the Israelites in virtually every way?
Our faith varying like a sine curve from day to day
One day praising the Lord and demonstrating we're all in
The next giving into temptation and turning from Him

But like the hall-of-fame quarterback, God never gives in
He has a "Hail Mary" that is spectacular, and we know He wins
He sends His Son to demonstrate His love, everlasting and true
Because in love, you just can't have someone else stand in for you

We can be on His team, and all we have to do is say yes to His Son
Say the prayer of repentance and admit He is the One
We don't have to be worried about our fate or be wary
All we have to do is be in the game and accept His "Hail Mary."

HEAVEN'S BIG ROOM

As I stood there in this enormous room, feeling terrified and small
I looked around and couldn't be sure it was a room at all
The walls were more like barricades of light and went on forever
My heart was pounding, and I hadn't felt like this, ever

Then I looked up, saw this big board, and gasped at the display
There for all to see were my sins from birth until today
They were scrolling across the screen in an endless show
The ones from just yesterday and ones so long ago

The sins of my life were all there in excruciating detail
The times I swore, lied, and cheated so as not to fail
The times I gossiped about others, including friends
The people I offended and never made amends

The people who were different that I ignored without a thought
The times I celebrated stealing something and not getting caught
The times I drank too much and justified going wild
The times, as a grownup, I acted like a child

The times I grumbled because things weren't going my way
Forgetting to thank God for each and every day
Turning away instead of helping those in need
Worshipping the money god with unabashed greed

Coveting the material possessions of my neighbor next door
His big house, fancy car, bank account, and more
Not stopping to realize I had also been immensely blessed
No matter, the grass was always greener, I guess

The times I refused to let humility be my guide
Bragging about accomplishments with unmitigated pride
Believing that somehow it was all under my control
And that I didn't need God to make me whole

The list went on and on and on until I could look no more
How was it that someone knew everything about me right to the core?
I thought I had lived a good life, a good person, all right
So why was I ready to run, ready to take flight?

My face turned red, my palms began to sweat, and my eyes to tear
All of my friends were watching with me, worsening my fear
I began to choke, the breaths coming short and strained
Where was I, and why was it so out of this world and strange?

Then I saw Him in the distance, dressed in white and all aglow
What was the penalty He had for me? I deserved it, I know
I remember reading that death is the wage of sin
I could not speak; no place to hide, no place to begin

As I was about to say I'm sorry for everything I'd done
He opened His arms and said, "Welcome home, son"
Tears welled up in my eyes, and I fell to my knees
I knew it was too late, but I said, "Lord, forgive me, please"

Then I noticed what looked like blood flowing down the screen
And as it did, it was erasing all my transgressions we had just seen
I stared in disbelief at what I did not understand
Then it dawned on me—the blood of the Son of Man!

And then they were there, thousands of angels, that is
They encircled us closely, and I knew they were His
The songs of joy they were singing were like nothing I'd heard
The lyrics, though, came straight from the Word

I was dumbfounded as I looked one last time at the board
And all I could get out was, "Thank You, Lord"
For the screen was blank, the sins were lost
Except for these words, "Debt paid on the cross"

Then I was awake. Was it a vision or just a dream?
The message was so vivid, though, I know what it means
It's a reminder that I am found where once I was lost
And that He gave it all up for me there on the cross.

I Stand at the Door

We go about our daily lives, and by the world's measures
We have it all—health, education, and many earthly treasures
We are not worried at all about what we'll drink or eat
Provisions aplenty just seem to cascade at our feet

But there's something missing; something we can't see
Maybe it's a better job, a new hobby, or an advanced degree
And so our search continues, a search frustrating and elusive
Some things work for a while but always end inconclusive

We think back to when our parents would tuck us in at night
We felt protected, loved, and knew everything was all right
We longed to recapture that feeling that we so missed
But the world is a scary place where comfort doesn't exist

Then one day, when least expected, comes the turnaround
Subtle, but like a lightning bolt that will knock you down
It is a spiritual awakening headed straight to the heart
It's something different, energizing, a brand new start

Jesus said, "I stand at the door and knock;" behold
He waits there for us to open our hearts, young and old
And when we do, He will come in and be with us all our days
Walking the corridors of life with us, teaching us His ways

It won't be a "knock-the-door-down knock," not at all
It's only in the quiet that you'll even hear His call
But if you answer and extend a heartfelt welcome to Him
You'll discover what it means to be spiritually born again

Most of the time, when someone knocks, and there's no response
That person will walk away, setting aside whatever his wants
But with Jesus, it will be quite different from experiences before
His knock will seem louder and louder until you answer the door

Jesus is the Patient One, and He's waiting at the door just for you
And even non-believers inherently know what they must do
Ask forgiveness for your sins and vow to follow Him
It's a life change initiated by opening the door and letting Him in.

IT'S THE HEART

Not the brain
Not the intellectual exercise of a genius IQ
Great minds often achieve worldly fame
But can't imagine how to be born anew

Not the eyes
What we see can be so deceiving
Satan, in many forms, master of disguise
But faith in the unseen can bring true believing

Not the mouth
Treachery lies in every corner, said and unsaid
Words better smothered, find their way out
Dispensing not compassion but distress instead

Not the ears
The truth is evident, but we don't listen
The Holy Spirit communicates, but we don't hear
Our internal receiver just seems to be missing

Not the circumcision
That under Jewish law was such a part
Rather an internal change was Paul's vision
A circumcision, all right, but one of the heart

The heart is where it all begins
Is it a hardened and sealed-off place
Or has it rejected Satan's call to sin
And freely accepted God's amazing grace?

When the Holy Spirit calls your name
And you're not sure just where to start
Invite Him in; accept the change
He will lead you if you just open your heart.

LEAN TOWARD THE LIGHT

Have you ever wondered why a barrel cactus leans to the south?
It's as if it's reaching for something it can't live without
Biologists will tell us it's the sun's life-sustaining rays
That the plant seeks and causes it to bend this way

It's no secret what plants need to flourish and grow
To rise up strong and dazzle us with their floral show
Fertilizer will be necessary regardless of terrain
And nothing survives without the blessing of rain

It got me thinking—what is it we need to spiritually grow?
What is it that nourishes our faith and feeds our soul?
What is it that makes us strong against the tempest wind
To resist Satan's urgings and the temptations of sin?

To the world, Jesus was a beacon, a light on the hill
When we turn to the light, we turn to our Father's will
In throwing off our chains, we find all we'll ever need
And experience the peace and joy of God's only seed

Like plants, we need nourishment feeding our roots
To move according to God's will and good works produce
The recipe for growth can only be found in God's Word
His instruction book shows us where and how we can serve

But growth in the Spirit cannot happen without godly rain
It cascades over our bodies and washes away the pain
By ourselves, it's not something we can set in place
This rain is the lifeblood of forgiveness, and we call it grace

So our growth has a lot in common with the plants you see
And we could probably further extrapolate this analogy
But suffice it to say that spiritually we'll be doing all right
If we just accept His grace and lean toward the light.

Purest of Gold

Gold has seemingly always been a treasure
Its beauty universally brings joy and pleasure
It provides the basis for most jewelry and rings
It says "love" and commitment more than anything

Westward expansion was fueled by the gold rush
People enduring impossible challenges to arrive first
Attacks along the way and mountains rising to the sky
In pursuit of this precious metal, many would die

King Solomon became rich through his collection of gold
And it adorns most architecture, whether recent or old
Streets of gold will highlight the new heaven on Earth
When all else fails, investors rely heavily on gold's worth

So gold has always been highly valued by every society
It's a status symbol, a major part of fashion and royalty
It is coveted equally by thugs and kings and queens
It's the object of criminal plans and vivid dreams

But gold ore must be purified by subjection to high heat
A thousand degrees may be required to make the process complete
And there may be several cycles depending on the purity required
And the extent to which the owner wants the gold admired

What's removed from the gold by heat is a slag called dross
If any remains, much of the metal's resplendence will be lost
Impurities like copper, zinc, and lead must be eliminated by the fire
If it's the luster and shine of pure gold to which you aspire

God intended Adam and Eve to be pure as gold in the Garden
But dross came in the form of a snake, and hearts hardened
Now God would have to take them and us through the fire
Purify us and sanctify us to be the children He desired

As a result, we will be challenged in many ways to make us pure
Eliminating dross like pride, lies, and lust to be sure
It will be painful at times to walk through the flames
But it will be made easier because we'll do it in Jesus' name

On each trip through the fire, we'll gradually purify
We will grow, move closer to God, and sanctify
We don't really know how many trips it will take
Until our lives are changed, and we live for His sake

On our own, we can never completely eliminate the dross
But Jesus provided a path to righteousness for us on the cross
So that, at the Judgment Throne, a new story will be told
When God looks at us, and all He'll see is the purest of gold.

Running After Me

I was just a child in a faithless family
Good people, but life spawned their apathy
I still had exposure to You in Sunday School
Learning how You lived and the Golden Rule

In those days, we still had religious education
And it provided us with a firm Christian foundation
We may have wandered as teenagers are want to do
But those biblical principles were the truth we knew

In college, it was all about me, leaving You behind
Meaningless philosophical discussions filled my mind
Secular humanism replaced You as my life's guide
I really didn't care why Jesus had suffered and died

Then there was the career, driven to succeed
And of a Savior, I just couldn't understand the need
Even though Your call was always in the background
Entwined in the worldview, I wasn't ready to be found

All this time, when I felt Your presence, I would flee
Yet, You were persistent and never gave up on me
You were always running toward me as I was running away
And that has made all the difference in who I am today

Even now, with the renewed hope I have in You
I sometimes fall back into the grip of the worldview
I forget all the blessings I've received, so plain to see
But when I turn around, You're still there, running after me

One day, I hope to be with You in the joy of paradise
Knowing that the tears will well up in my thankful eyes
Because I'll be free of the evil one and safe from all harm
Not running away, but running toward Your loving arms.

Spiritual Wheelchairs

Most of us have watched the Olympics on TV
Some may even have traveled to watch it directly
But have you ever tuned in to the para-version?
Wheelchair athletes overcoming every burden

Their dedication is not diminished at all by disability
They demonstrate amazing strength and awesome agility
"Can't" is routinely set aside in favor of already "Done"
Participation being way more important than who won

We sometimes feel great empathy for those handicapped
Thanking our lucky stars that that's not where we're at
But if we dwell on this a little, we'll see we're sadly mistaken
That we're all in a metaphorical wheelchair of our own making

Our wheelchair may not be visible to others, but it is to God
He clearly sees how desperate we are, how fatally flawed
We're handicapped in our own way if you think about it
Free will has put together our own wheelchair, bit by bit

We're not talking physical limitations here, but spiritual ones
Those that keep us from the Father when life on Earth is done
Our chairs are made up of lies, deceit, greed, and idols
Not praying to our Lord nor reading and studying the Bible

Every time we slander, we add another spoke to the wheel
As we do when we ignore someone in need of a healthy meal
Footrests are added when we look at another woman in lust
And the armrests come when our language is filled with cuss

But with all of our shortcomings, there is a blessing there
That one day, we'll stand tall on our feet and walk from that chair
Just as Jesus told the lame man to pick up his mat and walk away
Jesus will intervene, and we'll leave our chair on that glorious day

The wheelchair that represents all our imperfections will be gone
Standing in the presence of the Lord will welcome a new dawn
We'll be new beings in His eyes; no more need to sit in our shame
Our lives will be changed forever by the power of His name

So the next time you look at someone wheelchair-bound with pity
Keep in mind we have our own chair, and it's not pretty
We're not acceptable to God until we leave our sin vehicle behind
Only then can we spend eternity with Him for the rest of time.

THAT CHANGED EVERYTHING

To some, You were just a baby conceived like many before
To the Pharisees, You weren't the one they were looking for
You didn't fit the mold of the warrior, the all-conquering King
But when You arose from the dead, that changed everything.

To some, You were just a carpenter plying his trade
Handiwork creations perhaps proudly displayed
May have thought these were the only skills You'd bring
But when You arose from the dead, that changed everything

To some, You were just another prophet of zealous fame
One of those with a following, but no lasting name
Most couldn't imagine You could be the real thing
But when You arose from the dead, that changed everything

To some, You were just a preacher with tricks up Your sleeve
Nothing more than a magician, some would believe
At times even Your apostles would not Your praises sing
But when You arose from the dead, that changed everything

But now we know You came to Earth us sinners to save
Death would not have its way in that earthly grave
And now we know You were truly the Messiah, the King
Because when You arose from the dead, that changed everything.

THAT DAY

Lord, this is a troubled world we live in
And some days, it takes all we have not to give in
But when we're about to concede to the world's way
You take our memory back to That Day

That Day You struggled up to Golgotha hill
Lugging that cross according to Your Father's will
Beaten unmercifully with whips tearing at Your flesh
A time when Your apostles just weren't at their best

They didn't know You; that's what they said
Too afraid that they too might wind up dead
Watched in horror as You were nailed to the cross
Not understanding Your mission of saving the lost

The punishment You endured for our salvation
Providing a way for us out of eternal damnation
Thorns on Your head and nails through Your hands and feet
Blood that flowed to make God's redemption complete

You were faithful to the Father, and we were awed
Suffering the agony of a human, even though You were God
You could have stepped down from that cross at any moment
But that was not to be part of the lamb's atonement

By comparison, our troubles exact such a small price
We just stand in disbelief at Your loving sacrifice
Our worldly tribulations all fade to a place far away
If we just think about what transpired on That Day.

THE FOUNTAIN OF LIFE

The water from the fountain is refreshing, but still, I thirst
Things I pray will get better only seem to get worse
You, Lord, are the fountain of life, but I fear my last breath
I believe in eternity but still anguish over death

I try to be obedient to Your Word, but still, I sin
I pray for Your help, but the evil one often wins
You're the God of the Universe who made all things
Still, there are times I forget Your praises to sing

I'm showered by Your love and amazing grace
Yet I cater to the world and often run their race
I forget that You know every hair on my head
My trust should be in You, but I go my way instead

I want to be open, but I wear a mask
And I sometimes resist the things You ask
I'm completely unworthy of Your mercy
You offer eternal love, and yet I'm still thirsty

Lord, this is my prayer, to thirst no more
I long for the adventures You have in store
Give me the strength to climb every mountain
I want to drink it all in at Your fountain.

THREE SHEETS TO THE WIND

I am a sinner, and like many, I'd prefer to keep my sins hidden
But I wanted to know for sure my failings would be forgiven
So I decided to list them all on three sheets of paper
And present them all at the same time to my Lord and maker

The first sheet, if there is such a thing, might be called minor sins
Not minor in God's eyes, especially since they happen again and again
There in my youth, but still unchecked and continuing today
The page was full and wanted more, this disobedience resume

On this page were both sins of commission and omission
When help was clearly needed somewhere, it was missin'
People begging for some kind of assistance were left in the lurch
It can be inconvenient to stop when you're on your way to church

The second sheet listed those sins of the more serious kind
Their impact on others didn't diminish with the passage of time
Several were held close to the vest, and only God and I knew
The mistakes I had made that I could never really undo

This sheet was filled out by severity, not by the numbers
Things done in haste while my conscience slumbered
No thought at all as to whom or how it might affect
Driven by thoughtlessness and no measure of respect

Then there was the third sheet which was absolutely blank
And for that, I had the future and father time to thank
There was the expectation that more sin was in the wings
Because ever since the Garden, it's what our nature brings

Holding these three sheets, I asked for what I didn't deserve
That God would forgive me, and my place would be reserved
The tears that flowed were proof I was open and contrite
And completely at His mercy to make our relationship right

At that moment, a gust of wind swept the three sheets away
And in that instant, the aroma was sweeter than any bouquet
I knew only through the Son could God absolve my sin
But my prayer was answered in full by three sheets to the wind.

Undeserved Love

You, Lord, are Creator of the Universe and the Great I Am
You control everything by the sweep of Your mighty hand
The heavenly bodies move in accordance with Your command
Plants and animals exist only for the benefit of Your plan

When I think that every star may be the center of another galaxy
And that doesn't even account for the stars I can't see
Or consider the human body with all its complexity
I stand in awe of You and acknowledge Your sovereignty

Then I switch gears, Lord, and consider exactly what I am
On a ten-mile stretch of beach, just one tiny grain of sand
Such a small element in the cosmos, I'm largely out of view
And yet, somehow, You find me because that's what You do

I'm that grain of sand that washes back and forth with the tide
With no grounding at all unless I know You're by my side
And the fact that the Ruler of the Universe cares about me
Despite my self-centered, sinful life is hard to believe

Your love knows no limits; You proved that by sending Your Son
We just have to acknowledge what He said, "It is done"
That's an amazing love—showering down on us like spiritual rain
And the Great I Am offers it individually to each and every grain.

WASHED IN THE BLOOD

I have to admit I'm a bit of a neat freak when it comes to my car
But compared to others, I may not be as nitpicky or go as far
Living here in the desert brings its own challenge in keeping it clean
Blowing dust and drops of rain require almost daily hygiene

And keeping the outside looking spiffy is only half the chore
Take a peek inside, and you'll find there's a whole lot more
A part of everything you walk on finds a home on the floor mat
Kids, animals, and spilled drinks may leave their own impact

Your car may look stunning on the outside to passersby
But you might get a different impression if you look inside
Accumulated dust and dirt may be wanting for a vacuum or wash
And cleanliness will only come with added effort and cost

Isn't this a great analogy for us in how we live day-to-day?
Where cosmetologists are more than happy to show us the way
Where we can spend thousands on makeup, hair, and skin cream
To accomplish that Hollywood look for which we can only dream

But when someone really looks at the inside of us, what's there?
Is it as delightful to look at as maybe our dress, jewelry, or hair?
Do you think the Lord would be pleased with what He sees inside?
At what He witnesses going on unabated in our heart and mind

Over and over again, He has told us His concern is our heart
So what do we do about it; where to make a fresh start
How do we clean up the inside so that others clearly see
We're not even close to the same individual we used to be

With God's help, we can become less conceited, more humble
More willing to help others who lose their way and stumble
More amenable to listening and learning instead of holding court
Knocking down walls that once protected our personal fort

We can clean out our "human car" one change, one day at a time
And slowly remove all traces of life's collection of dirt and grime
Going to the Lord each day to give thanks and ask He forgive
Creating a sparkling new image, a new perspective on how to live

But even with our best efforts, we're still unclean outside and in
It's built into our nature, and on our own, we can't overcome sin
We must traverse God's "human wash," that is, Jesus Christ
Only His blood can wash us clean because He paid the ultimate price

People will take notice that you're different and looking new
They'll see you don't do things the way you used to
They'll wonder where you obtained this shiny new attitude
And you can tell them your Lord, Jesus Christ, gave it to you

They won't understand at first what His death and resurrection meant
But we'll tell them it was the Father's love for which Jesus was sent
That we come to Him like a car just driven through the mud
And inside and out, we'll be washed clean by our Savior's blood

The beauty of this wash is it costs us nothing; it's absolutely free
It's a gift the Lord made available to everyone, including you and me
And when we accept, we shine before the Father, perfect in every way
Jesus Himself is there to intercede for us on that Judgment Day.

WHITE AS SNOW

It's disgusting when I look out and see trash everywhere
Walls painted with graffiti; not an empty space to spare
Beer bottles and tire rubber scattered along the road
And yards overgrown as if there's no neighborhood code

Just when you think that it's always going to be this way
The heavens rain down with an awesome display
Like a worn-down shack that transforms to a chateau
The world is renewed with a fresh blanket of snow

There's nothing quite as cleansing as new-fallen snow
For a few hours, it puts a mask on all the ugliness below
Mother Nature, untouched by even one set of tracks
Glistens with a beauty and softness humanity lacks

It may be cold outside, but the snow warms the heart
All things are made fresh, and the world gets a new start
All you can do is step back and admire a world made new
It's energizing and uplifting through and through

It brings back memories of when you were a child
Snowball fights, snow angels, and all the smiles
For just a while, setting aside all the ugly
Making even the cold seem warm and cuddly

That's what God's grace is like, raining down on us below
Soft and invigorating like a blanket of freshly fallen snow
It covers all our shortcomings, transgressions, and sins
The ugly is painted white, with another chance to begin

Our Lord's death on the cross was an ugly testament to man
He said they know not what they do; they don't understand
But He provided a way for us, and only now do we know
That when we come to Him, we're seen white as snow.

Faith—Trust

"Truly I tell you, if you have faith as small as a mustard seed, you can say to this mountain, 'Move from here to there,' and it will move. Nothing will be impossible for you" (Matthew 17:20, NIV).

"Trust in the Lord with all your heart and lean not on your own understanding; in all your ways submit to him, and he will make your paths straight" (Proverbs 3:5–6, NIV).

BE A PETER AND STEP OUT OF THE BOAT

Peter was strong in character, ambitious, and outspoken
But he was missing when his Lord's body was beaten and broken
So why did Jesus look around at His followers, take stock
And decide that this flawed disciple would be His rock

It all goes back to his faith being tested on Galilee, I think
The only one stepping out of the boat, not expecting to sink
Peter would go on to be the leader Christ needed and expected
Emboldened by the Holy Spirit and moved by Jesus resurrected

So what impact does this have on us who proclaim to follow Christ?
What will we do to spread the gospel, and at what price?
Are we doing our part to bring people to the streets of gold?
Or are we making excuses—no skills and way too old?

I think, like those twelve, we need a change of mind
And when we do that, here's what I believe we'll find
The tasks He places before us will surely seem small
Compared to the challenges He set before Peter and Paul

We might be a little tentative when we take that first step
But faith will carry us across the water if we just accept
That He is with us each and every step of the way
That His power will calm the storm and all fears allay

We're not going to be martyred like those fishers of men
But I believe He's going to call on us again and again
When the others sit back and wait for the story to be wrote
Don't wait for someone else; be a Peter and step out of the boat.

BUTTERFLY

It all starts inconsequentially with the egg deposited on a leaf
It's such a small beginning it's hardly visible to the naked eye
But what's about to happen is almost beyond belief
It's a transformation that will absolutely amaze and mystify

In short order, this multi-legged creature appears before our eyes
Its voracious appetite devours the leaf it's on and many, many more
It grows rapidly to four or five times its original size
But this caterpillar gives us no hint of the change that's in store

Like us humans, after we've eaten too much, the caterpillar rests
He wraps himself up in this blanket which we call a cocoon
We might think there's nothing happening, just time to digest
But a dramatic change is coming, and it's coming soon

The cocoon begins to open, and a completely new creature appears
It's nothing at all like the caterpillar; it seems almost like magic
We're not quite sure what to expect as the big moment nears
But the beautiful butterfly emerging is both amazing and dramatic

There's another kind of transformation that will much more astound
The butterfly is a metaphor for how the unbeliever can change
The egg represents just the beginning of a new life found
Just listening passively to the message begins to loosen the chains

The caterpillar represents an intense period of studying God's Word
A voracious appetite develops for understanding everything in the Bible
He learns to listen to instruction coming directly from the Lord
His passion for knowledge of Jesus Christ, the Savior, has no rival

The cocoon stage represents a time of dramatic change and reflection
Connecting the understanding of the mind with acceptance of the heart
Marveling that God would come to Earth and save us by resurrection
And we have to do very little—just by accepting His gift, we do our part

The butterfly emerges and spreads its wings like an opening flower
It's a scene that enthralls, full of wonder, a truly spectacular feat
But not nearly as spectacular as the impact of the Holy Spirit's power
The one that indwells and makes the believer's transformation complete

Like the butterfly, this emerging believer is a completely different type
More compassionate, peaceful; it's the Lord he wants to glorify
He's shut out all the worldly din—the distortions, the lies, and the hype
He's been transformed through the blood of Christ; he's a butterfly.

COMPLETE TRUST

In life, there are so many things where trust is a given
Someone or something we count on as part of livin'
We believe that the plane we're in will not come down
Or that other drivers will not run the red lights in town

We trust that the bank will not steal our money
That the rain will give way to days that are sunny
That the cruise ship we're on will not sink
And that we'll be all right if we trust our instincts

The running back trusts his linemen to open a hole
And the basketball player relies on the pick and roll
When the game's on the line, the team trusts its star
Because he's the one who brought them this far

We place our money in a trust for the next generation
To give them a future with a solid foundation
By working hard, we trust we'll stay employed
And continue the lifestyle that we've so enjoyed

There is some measure of trust wherever we turn
From child to adult, it's something we learn
In its absence, we're nothing but a chaotic society
Living in fear and distrust, paralyzed by anxiety

But when it comes to God, the notion seems like a crutch
Even though our currency says "In God We Trust"
When times are good, we rely on our own control
But in tough times, there are no atheists in the foxhole

I think we act like this because we don't truly believe
That God's awesome power created everything we see
That He is concerned about our life—every detail
That He is with us every day, every hour without fail

I have to admit there are times when I put my trust in me
And my short-term view of how things should be
My limitations are evident; I just can't comprehend
How I can follow the unknowns of God's perfect plan

So I go my own way; I'm so much a work in progress
But I know deep in my heart that I'll never have success
Until I set aside my own free will, listen, and adjust
Placing all my confidence in the only one I can trust

If I can just do that, I know I'll spend eternity with Him
Even though my life is one of disobedience and sin
It's been a long-time coming, but I'm learning it's a must
That only in Him and His grace can I have complete trust.

FAITH METER

We have meters for just about everything, a full repertoire
Gas gauges, odometers, and speedometers for our car
Meters for water usage and the electricity our house needs
Altimeters for airplanes as well as indicators for airspeed

Thermometers tell us temperature, whether hot or cold
That pedometer device records miles walked, young or old
Voltmeters and ammeters measure electrical flow
And ohmmeters measure resistance to it, high or low

So I was wondering what would a meter for our faith look like.
Even the most ardent believer can see his faith fall or spike
And, in the foxhole, even the atheist will consider prayer a must
The scale runs from rejection through doubt to complete trust

Satan himself wants to move us closer to the rejection end
While God positions Himself on the other as our savior friend
Being humanly flawed, most of us move up and down this scale
Angry with God one day; the next, seeing His love never fails

When we make quiet time available each day to our Lord
We move closer to trust, as we do when we're in His Word
When times are difficult, and we turn our backs, shut Him out
That's when we move down the scale to the area of doubt

And Satan is always there with his lies and deception
Using his tricks of discouragement to move us toward rejection
We know we displease our Father when we listen to him
But he keeps tempting us, and we capitulate again and again

So how's your faith meter doing? Are you pleased to show it?
Or, when you're around others, would they even know it?
Would they know you put your trust in God in all you do?
Or, by your everyday action, would they not have a clue?

Like the automotive tachometer that, in the extreme, redlines
Are you working to be at the trust end of the scale at all times?
That's where God wants us to be, as demonstrated by Paul and Peter
Doing everything we can to live at the trust end of the faith meter.

FLY LIKE AN EAGLE

Eagles are clearly one of our most majestic birds
Their maneuvers in the sky astound beyond words
Despite their awesome wingspan and impressive size
No wing movement is needed to dramatically fall or rise

They've learned to dance on the air like a Baryshnikov ballet
It could be put to music, this phenomenal display
They wing their way through the blue with no effort at all
It's as smooth as a Viennese waltz at a gala ball

Eagles always nest in high places, either cliffs or trees
But how do the eaglets acquire this soaring expertise?
How do they discover the elegance when it's their turn?
And what are the baby steps it takes to learn?

It's a lot like a baby venturing out to take his first steps
It involves a very short distance and many, many reps
The eaglet will hop from branch to branch with wings aflap
Then short flights to more distant branches and back

Then finally, with wings fully extended, it's a leap of faith
And he's off to the wind to meet destiny's fate
He is obligated to leave the security of his parents' nest
And set out on his own adventure, his personal quest

He still has to learn the intricacies of managing the thermals
Floating on the updrafts until it's second nature and normal
Doing and being everything God imagined him to be
And setting a standard of beauty and unequaled majesty

Isn't this a great analogy for what God expects of us?
Our days were never intended to be quite superfluous
We're not meant to spend our lifetime in our comfort zone
Instead, we must spread our wings and strike out on our own

Like the eaglet, it may take a number of small beginnings
Until we feel secure to take on the world and spread our wings
Until we can learn how to master the downs and enjoy the lifts
Appreciating what life has to offer and accepting the gifts

So the next time you see an eagle floating on the air
Imagine how wonderful life could be with you up there
You may be poor, but your days can still be regal
If you just spread your wings and fly like an eagle.

GOD'S GOT THIS

Life is full of challenges, and the answers can be few
Experts are everywhere, delighted to tell us what to do
And we like to think for every problem a solution exists
The popular response today being, "I got this"

Another popular mantra is the phrase git 'er done
Implying it's all up to us; we don't need anyone
It's a bit like a fairy tale and about as fictitious
When we strut our stuff and proclaim, "I got this"

But we were not created to go it on our own
Despite the bravado for which our culture is known
Sometimes we cannot find the strength within ourself
It takes another source from whence comes our help

Often there are people we know offering a helping hand
And it won't diminish our worth or disrupt our plan
If we just accept their help and work together
To lessen the burden and make the outcome better

But sometimes the obstacle we face is more mountain than hill
It just overwhelms our ability and destroys our will
In times like this, there's someone we can trust
Seeking Him in prayer is more than a good idea; it's a must

God is there for us every day, every minute, and every hour
We can come to Him and tap into His awesome power
Regardless of the situation, small problem or big crisis
We can turn to Him and be assured, "He's got this"

He knows every hair on our head, every thought, every mistake
He's there in the good times and through the heartache
When you've exhausted all options despite intense analysis
Take it up with the Lord because you know "God's got this."

God's GPS

I'm a baby boomer, and it's not foreign for us to look at a map
But succeeding generations simply find the appropriate app
Even us boomers have become quite dependent on the GPS
Having someone tell you where to turn is nearly effortless

We make our turns as instructed without the slightest resistance
No reason to question that little dashboard assistant
It's only when the signal gets lost and we discover we are too
That we may have to resort to the old ways instead of the new

I think God has a GPS system as well, not relying on human technology
Directing humans instead of cars relies on a different methodology
Instructions so subtle that unless you listen carefully, you'll not hear
But if you do, you'll never be lost; your way will be clear

Directions for life always begin with **God's Prayer System**, His GPS
And if we know how to access it, we are definitely blessed
It works like this; we send up prayers to Him to help us decide
When to turn, make a change, and put away our selfish pride

God's GPS is way more sophisticated than anything you can buy
After a while, you'll just do as He says without asking why
His instruction comes via the Holy Spirit, your built-in receiver
His wise counsel helps us resist misdirection from the Deceiver

You'll be tempted to turn away and take the shortcut at times
But shortcuts are usually not what your Lord and Savior has in mind
And after seeing that where He's taking you is all for the best
You'll be glad you installed in your heart God's GPS.

HOLDING HANDS WITH GOD

I remember when everything in life was new
And I couldn't be sure who or what to hold onto
Just a kid, there was much I didn't understand
But I always had the security of my father's hand

That hand was always there to guide me through the crowd
Bringing calm to an atmosphere overwhelming and loud
There was safety as I reached for his hand to direct my feet
Avoid the rushing cars and escort me across the street

In childhood, that hand often pulled me back from danger
And protected me from the unknown of an approaching stranger
One of the scariest times was in the dead of night
That touch was so calming and always soothed my fright

Holding hands with my first love was a moment of bliss
Often followed in short measure with that first kiss
Holding hands at the altar is a time to remember
A feeling of oneness to cherish then and forever

But there's the hand of another to which none can compare
And it's been there steering my choices year after year
There were times I'd let go and move ahead on my own
But when trouble came, I'd look for God's hand to hold

I've strayed off the path many times, wandering lost and alone
I'm so thankful His hand was there, the one I've always known
The one that brings me back and takes away all anxiety
The one I want to hold onto through all eternity

My earthly father's hand was there, just the right touch
When I look back, I appreciated its comfort oh so much
But I can't meet life's challenges now and fulfill God's plan
Unless I walk with Him and work with Him, holding hands

His gentle hand has guided me through times, good and bad
The times of great rejoicing and the times of the "Great Sad"
I don't need Him just when there are troubles to overcome
I'm holding hands with Him every hour until my days are done.

LIVING WITH ADVENTURE

Routine seems to be a good thing, especially at the start
It denotes comfort, order, and predictability
But over time, it becomes a rut right through the heart
Often the root of depression, anger, and irritability

Jesus said, "I come that they may have life abundantly"
There's nothing in that statement that suggests routine
We were meant to have a life that's open-ended and free
Not one that's filled with boredom and lack of a dream

Life should be full of adventure and, yes, risk
Trying something that some folks might call wild
Learning something new, fulfilling a lifelong wish
Adding zest and excitement, like that of a child

Routine can be comfortable because there's no surprise
But it's not living the way God intended us to
Just as Christmas morning lights up a child's eyes
Our lives should be filled with wonder at all things new

I've often found myself caught up in the power of routine
Each day of the week looking just like the week before
Going through life like a robot; a repetitive machine
And only with trepidation peering behind the closed door

We all know that a certain amount of routine is necessary
Otherwise, our world descends into complete chaos
But we need to push back against the mundane and ordinary
And fill our lives with adventure no matter the cost

We are born with a thirst like a man lost in the desert
We're searching for water, but it's not H2O
God promised us living water to deal with the hurt
The Holy Spirit giving us adventure only God can bestow

So stay in the security of that daily rut, if you must
But if you do, I think the end will come with much regret
That you didn't live according to God's plan, didn't trust
Missing the opportunities between every sunrise and sunset.

NOTHING SEEMS TO MATTER BUT EVERYTHING DOES

For those of us who were raised in gentler times
What's going on today seems completely misaligned
Fraud is everywhere, and we've split into factions of "me"
We seem to have lost any semblance of national unity

We're eroding the Christian values our country was founded on
Walking away from the triune—Father, Holy Spirit, and Son
The national news is depressing, bordering on out-and-out lies
Anarchy, riots, and complete disrespect for the law are on the rise

We don't debate the issues anymore, just shout each other down
Praise and smiles have been replaced by accusation and frown
You may feel your part in all this doesn't matter at all
The things you can do so inconsequential, their effect so small

You may be just a working stiff trying to live the American dream
You'll not be seen on the evening news, but you're mainstream
While the news media may not grant an opportunity for your view
There's someone watching and monitoring everything you do

So if you've fallen into the trap that nothing matters
That your voice just gets lost in all the political chatter
You can be an army of one in your own neighborhood
Showing kindness, helpfulness, and real brotherhood

Generally, we are unable to do the newsworthy big things
But when we attend to the little ones, God's heart sings
There are so many opportunities, too numerous to mention
But if they're on your heart, you need to give them your attention

The Lord of the Universe is watching, and He cares
All the things you do or don't do in His name, He's aware
One day you'll come before the throne and give an account
Of all the things you've done for others or those you left out

Good deeds may not be rewarded on Earth; you understand
But your reward in heaven comes directly from the Father's hand
So even if your impact feels negligible, keep the faith because
While it may seem that nothing matters, everything does.

SEEDS OF DOUBT

Are you a Christian whose faith is pretty small?
You believe there is a God, but that's about all
You come to God mostly in troubled times
But forget about Him when everything's fine

Your prayers are short; requisitions are rehearsed
You don't expect answers and prepare for the worst
You may really wonder if there is a heaven or hell
And there just seems to be so many doubts to dispel

If we're honest, we all have some measure of doubt
And our culture uses every trick to get us to sell out
But God is bigger than anything they can produce
And He is waiting for you to turn His power loose

The smallest seed in biblical times was the mustard seed
Yet it could grow, with nourishment, into a small tree
Big enough that birds could come and perch on a branch
Build a nest there and make a home if given a chance

So even faith that's less resistant to sin's temptation
Can, with time, grow strong enough to handle every situation
And provide sanctuary for those who would come to Christ
The Holy Spirit's power bringing their faith to new heights

Jesus said in His teaching, "Nothing is impossible with God"
Bring your petitions to Him and prepare to be awed
Without Him, even the smartest man can do nothing at all
But even the weakest faith can grow and answer His call

So regardless of where you are today in your faith walk
You, too, can become as solid as Peter, the Rock
From that small seed, great branches can sprout
And remove any and all traces of the seeds of doubt.

Ship of Faith

What if God asked you to do something considered borderline insane?
Would you do it even if it seemed the loss might far outweigh the gain?
What if you weren't skilled and didn't understand the work to be done
And you had some doubts about the outcome or the victory to be won?

Has God ever asked you to do something that seemed beyond your reach?
Maybe something you didn't think you could learn, let alone teach
Did you react by standing firm, using the age-old question, "Why me?"
Or did you get busy with the task at hand for an outcome you could not see?

Think about Noah, building this monstrous ark high on a hill, with no water near
An awesome task even for a young man, but Noah was up in years
Even if he had some shipbuilding experience, it was nothing on this scale
But he set to the task, knowing that God would not allow him to fail

It's hard to imagine he did not suffer rejection, persecution, and ridicule
But when it was all done, and the Lord had His way, who was the fool?
It took years for Noah to obey, put up with the insults, and complete the task
I'm guessing he had his doubts right to the end about what God had asked

But the door was open for Noah and his family, and he chose to walk through
Do you do the same when the door is flung wide open for you?
It must have been sweet vindication for Noah and joy he could not restrain
When the clouds formed, the thunder struck, and it began to rain

So how do we respond when the task is great to which we've been called?
Do we say the task is too hard, the water's too deep, or the mountain's too tall
Or do we plunge right in obediently, praying that the Lord will show us the way
And that He will provide the lamp at our feet on even the darkest day?

What Noah built was more than a floating zoo; it was a monumental ship of faith
The ship's size alone was a testament to the perseverance it would take
Noah had built his trust on God's promise that his family would be saved
That they would survive the battering of the waves and the watery grave

How's your ship of faith doing? Have you secured everything to the main beam?
That would be Jesus Christ, holding it all together in even stormy extremes
Will your ship even stay upright and stable when the ocean pounds its side?
When the persecution comes, will the Lord be your strength and your guide?

Will you stand firm when the world attacks you and mocks your beliefs?
Or will your ship end up on the rocks and be destroyed on the reefs?
God gave detailed instructions to Noah on how to build a great ark
Likewise, the Bible shows us how to follow Jesus and leave our mark

All we have to do is heed His instructions, trust, and obey
And our ship will be on solid ground when the waters go away
Like Noah, whose ship came to rest on Ararat in answer to prayer
Our Lord will bring us safely home, and we'll anchor there.

Spiritual Glasses

The Bible tells us to put on the full armor of God to metaphorically speak
The breastplate of righteousness and the shield of faith for the weak
The sword of the Spirit, the belt of truth, and the helmet of salvation
Once suited up for the warfare to come, praying in all situations

But if we're to resist Satan in all his forms, in all his disguises
We need to add something else to defeat the one God despises
It's not Excalibur, the white horse, or arrows for the coming clashes
You may be surprised that it's not a weapon, but a form of glasses

Glasses, you say, are you feeling all right, or are you out of your mind?
But these are no ordinary glasses; they're quite a different kind
They're not reading glasses or those that protect your eyes from the sun
They're not bifocals or transition lenses with stylish frames overdone

These glasses have a focus that's not on the things of today
They won't let the distractions or troubles of Earth get in the way
These are spiritual glasses that will put you on bended knee
And they're focused not on this life but the life to come—eternity

They're the same glasses David wore when he faced the Philistine giant
It was not on his power but on the Lord's that he was totally reliant
So it was with Daniel, trusting in the Lord to close the lion's jaws
And rendering it impossible for the lion to strike with his powerful claws

Then there's Shadrach, Meshach, and Abednego in the furnace of fire
Saved from a nasty death even though the flames roared higher
And don't you think Moses wore the glasses when God parted the sea
And then collapsed it on the Egyptians, drowning their invincibility

Did you not see the glasses Jesus wore while hanging from the cross?
Surely, they allowed Him to see the victory over death, not the loss
To see that His time at the right hand of the Father was near
That His ascension was at hand; a vision made perfectly clear

When we put on these glasses, we see things not of this Earth
But the New Jerusalem, eternity, and what God's promises are worth
We can look beyond all our fears, challenges, and all other things
Focus on the cross, God's will, and the power He brings

So if you're being tossed around like the waves on the sea
Maybe your relationship with the Lord isn't what it's supposed to be
If your life is in turmoil and you find it difficult to rise from the ashes
Maybe it's time to focus on Him and put on those spiritual glasses.

THE FLASHLIGHT

In writing poetry, I'm always searching for a good metaphor
Here's one I ran across I'd never thought about before
It comes with a simple message, but also so profound
You may laugh initially, but I think you'll come around

This item shines into the darkness, illuminating the night
It's as common as anything we own; it's the flashlight
During the day, it's not needed; the sun provides light for all
But it is absolutely essential when the curtain of darkness falls

It is powered by one or more batteries, depending on its size
When the power is no more, then the flashlight dies
Unlike the flashlight, God's power is infinite and never dims
And if we're wise, we'll always stay connected to Him

In the flashlight, the bulb is always connected to the battery
Likewise, Jesus is connected to the Father for all eternity
As the flashlight needs both the bulb and the battery for power
We need both the Father and the Son every day and every hour

The flashlight needs one more thing to work—the switch
And so does your faith, if your spiritual life is to be rich
When you flip the switch and ask Jesus to be your lifeline
The Holy Spirit comes and powers your being to brightly shine

Like the flashlight, you'll be able to illuminate a dark world
Allowing the fruit of the Spirit to be shown like a flag unfurled
Everyone will know you're not perfect, just trying to do right
Your power won't come from a battery but from the God of light.

THE GREAT PROVIDER

Did you ever notice how all the animals get along just fine?
Without any plan for their next meal or if it's on time
The robin hops along the ground until he finds a worm
And the rabbit comes out at dusk, the coyote has learned

The hummingbird finds nectar by hovering at each flower
And watching a pelican fish is a study in finesse and power
The squirrel is perhaps the most ingenious of them all
Storing up pine nuts for the Winter before the end of Fall

The big cats wait for the deer to fall off his guard
So that finding and subduing his next meal is not that hard
Raptors rely on aerial acrobatics and keen eyesight
To capture prey in their strong talons and take to flight

The animals just seem to go about business without stress
Doing what they know how to do and giving it their best
Tomorrow is not even on their radar screen or purview
Their only concern is today and the things they must do

Humans, on the other hand, worry about their health
What they will wear; what they will eat, and their wealth
There seems to be no end to all the things they worry about
With every turn in circumstances comes a measure of doubt

Jesus told His followers not to worry about tomorrow
Each day will have its own challenges and sorrow
Like the birds of the air who don't sow, reap, or store
Address each morning at dawn and not a minute before

We seem to go through life as if worry were a must
And we can trace it all back to a lack of complete trust
He has control of it all, and He will always provide
And all we have to do is keep Him close by our side

So, take a cue from the animal kingdom and their daily routine
Empty that worry closet and start each day fresh and clean
Your attitude will be better and your burden lighter
If you turn it all over to the Great Provider.

THE PUZZLE

Have you ever worked on a jigsaw puzzle to pass the time?
You know, the 500-piece or 1000-piece kind?
Where it's the picture on the box you're trying to recreate
And it involves equal parts of motivate and exasperate

You usually start with piecing together the border
By doing this, you bring some structure to this disorder
From then on, it's finding pieces of the same color scheme
That you try to hook together to match the box scene

But how successful would you be if you had no picture?
Wouldn't you be frustrated with such a chaotic mixture?
And after minutes turned to hours with precious little success
Wouldn't you want someone to help you out with this mess?

Isn't that a lot like life as we try to put the pieces together?
Positioning one piece at a time to make the whole look better
And we don't know what the final picture will look like
We can only hope for a life that reaches the highest heights

But don't you know there's someone with every piece in hand?
Only He knows which pieces to hand you for His perfect plan
And we don't have to know how it all matches; how it ends
We just have to take the first step, place a piece, and begin

It's been said you don't have to have the whole staircase in mind
To, in faith, take that first step and begin your climb
So pick up that first piece and place it on the table
Listen to God; you may not have a clue, but He is able

We must be careful not to force a piece where it doesn't belong
Recognizing that our inclination to go it alone is all wrong
Because any piece that's misplaced affects the final whole
Even if it feels good for a short time to be in control

But if you follow His will, taking it one day, one piece at a time
There's no obstacle you can't overcome or mountain you can't climb
Gradually, the picture you're constructing will come into view
And you'll experience the wonderful life God created for you

The puzzle that's life is all put together in God's flawless plan
He holds the finished picture on the box; it's in His hand
There will be times when the piece He's giving doesn't seem to fit
But maybe all you had to do was trust in Him and just turn it a bit

When you step back and know you've completed the scene
God's power will reveal blessings like you've never seen
You'll look back on a life with all the pieces in place
And you'll understand the impact of His amazing grace.

Today Is a Gift

Today is a gift
A blessing for sure
Will it be one to treasure
Or just another to endure?

Each day is an opportunity
The Lord has sent your way
Will you use it wisely
Or just let it slip away?

Time is racing forward
This day will soon be done
Will you fill the fleeting minute
With a full sixty seconds run?

Will you be receptive
To what God has in store?
Or will you go your own way
Like so many times before?

Will you appreciate the beauty
Of flowers, mountain, and brook?
Or will you be so engrossed
You fail to even look?

Will you encourage a friend
Not wasting another minute?
Or will you forget how they enrich your life
And how glad you are they're in it?

Will you be a blessing
To someone less fortunate than you?
Or will you just walk away
Convinced there's nothing you can do?

Will you look to the heavens
And contemplate God's awesome power
Be grateful that He walks with you
Each second, each minute, each hour?

Will today be the day
When you say, "Yes, Lord, Yes"
I'm following You
With a heart full of thankfulness?

What if somehow you knew
That today was your last day?
Would you have a list of regrets
About what you failed to do or say?

Don't let this day pass
The sand is trickling through
Today is a gift
From our Lord to you.

WATER TO WINE

The wedding at Cana is one of my favorite Bible stories
It seems to be about hospitality, but it's about God's glory
It seemed that everything was in order, proceeding just fine
Until the host discovered he had run out of wine

On the surface, this story highlights a normal worldly concern
When Mary makes Jesus aware of what she had learned
But when Jesus' response to her request was, "It's not my time"
It was certain He wasn't talking about the shortage of wine

Rather, He was talking about the mission He'd been given by God
Mary knew that those present would be astounded, even awed
That's why she says, "Do whatever he tells you to do"
Knowing water to wine was just a part of the Good News

While the water-to-wine miracle has been told and retold
The timeless message that it brings just never grows old
But look around; God is performing miracles every day
And He's using bad situations as heaven's gateway

I'll give you a few examples, but it barely scratches the surface
Of all the bad-to-good situations that we might want to list
In some cases, it doesn't even seem like God's involved at all
But be assured He's always there answering the call

Let's start with Lou Gehrig, one of the greatest of all time
How motivating was it to others, this story of water to wine?
Knowing at the peak of his baseball career, he would not long survive
As ALS was taking its toll, he proclaimed to be the luckiest man alive

How about Travis Freeman, a very good football player who lost his sight
In a short forty-eight hours, he went from 20/20 to seeing nothing but night
Through faith, he became the first blind football player to actually play
And with a PhD, he continues to motivate and inspire others to this day

Then there's Clebe McClary, a Vietnam vet who lost an arm and an eye
After forty surgeries, if he'd given up, you'd understand why
But the Lord wouldn't let him go; he wasn't out of time
Today he's a motivational speaker and turning water to wine

Patrick Knight was having a successful career and a very normal life
Until his brother-in-law went on a rampage, killing his pregnant wife
He also was shot several times, and death seemed a virtual certainty
But today, he spends time helping others overcome adversity

There are many examples of water to wine in God's plan
Saul, the Christian persecutor, who became His leading man
Moses, the one with the speech impediment, freed his people
A relationship with God no other human has ever equaled

Job's hardships were incredible, taking him to the limits of his faith
Satan attempting to show God he could turn his devotion to hate
But Job, even near death, continued to walk the faith line
And God rewarded him by once again turning water to wine

But the greatest example of water to wine ever told
Was Christ suffering and dying on the cross for all to behold
Who, with His resurrection, changed the world as the author
Of the only path to righteousness and eternity with the Father

So, if you're struggling with some obstacle that seems insurmountable
Know that you can tap into the One whose blessings are bountiful
It may not happen as you would want or probably in your time
But be assured the God of the Universe still turns water into wine.

WEAVING LIVES

The other night, in my dreams, I saw the Weaver
His looms were humming for every believer
The tapestries were masterpieces to behold
Intricately interwoven threads of silver and gold

I knew in an instant these were lives He was spinning
Some tapestries were nearly finished, some just beginning
The Master sat at the controls in this heavenly ballet
And smiled with each new soul that came His way

I looked a little closer and saw the tapestry for me
But it pleased me not in the least for what I could see
Yes, like the others, there was the finely crafted part
But there was also something there that broke my heart

The silver and gold were strung together in elegance
Flawlessly they moved together like some mysterious dance
But every now and then in the pattern was a major flaw
All of this beauty was brought down by the ugliness I saw

I stood there trying to understand what went wrong
Why didn't this section of threads seem to belong?
Then it hit me why these flaws so damaged the whole
These were the times in my life when I insisted on control

There were many times when I wouldn't listen to His voice
Mistakenly thinking what I had in mind was a better choice
He gave me free will, and I too often exercise that blessing
The results, though, which benefit no one, are distressing

Suddenly I was awake and thinking about the dream
Its meaning wasn't subtle; it was like a laser beam
Trust in Him every minute, every hour, every day
Listen to that voice, take it to heart, and obey

If I do all that, my life tapestry will be beautiful for all to see
And they'll know just who put it all together for me
Those flaws will give way to silver and gold if I'm wise
And allow the Lord to do what He does best, weaving lives.

WHAT ONLY GOD CAN SEE

In 1965, Doris Day had a hit entitled "Qué Será Será"
Translated, it means "what will be will be"
It's looking ahead at life, the unassembled jigsaw
And wondering how the pieces will become me

I don't think the song was written with any theology in mind
It does point out that we cannot envision even life's next phase
That it's all out of our control; we're completely blind
And haven't we found that to be true all of our days?

Life is full of twists and turns, sudden changes in direction
We don't see them coming, but with each, we adapt
Roadblocks rise up before us, and we must make a new selection
We head out on a new course, never looking back

So, is our life just a series of stop-and-go events?
Is there no set plan, just a collection of happenstance?
Where we are right now, does it make any sense?
Or, only in the end do we realize it was all one masterful dance?

Our life has been choreographed in every detail by the Master
We can't see around the next corner, but He can
We can't see what's over the next hill, whether sorrow or laughter
And it's often only in retrospect that we can fully understand

Even before the womb, His divine purpose He was bringing
He sees all and knows all; on that, you can depend
God sees your life from the end to the beginning
Rather than the way we see things, from beginning to end

It's almost like we're in chapter three and God's in twenty-one
It's only in hindsight we can see He was always in control
We may fight Him for a while, but eventually, we succumb
And understand why we must submit, body and soul

Our God is a great big God, creator, and ruler of the Universe
But He's also a personal God who cares deeply about you and me
Each one of us was brought into this world for a specific purpose
Only through following His will can we be who we were created to be

So, maybe that old song has it right, we don't know what our life will be
But, in those hours of quiet, when we can hear His voice
If we just listen and obey, the shackles will fall, and we'll be set free
Worry will fade; we'll bow to what only God can see and rejoice.

JOY—PEACE

"You will go out in joy and be led forth in peace; the mountains and hills will burst into song before you, and all the trees of the field will clap their hands" (Isaiah 55:12, NIV).

"Do not be anxious about anything, but in every situation, by prayer and petition, with thanksgiving, present your requests to God. And the peace of God, which transcends all understanding, will guard your hearts and your minds in Christ Jesus" (Philippians 4:6–7, NIV).

A WALK IN THE RAIN

What is it about running water that so enthralls?
Is it an adjunct of nature that seems to quietly call?
What is it that gives us a sense of calm and peace
Allowing us to just lay back and our worries release?

Why is it almost mystic to stroll along the ocean?
Or standing next to Niagara Falls, like a love potion?
Why does an all-day rain cleanse not only Earth
But also refresh our longing soul, like a rebirth?

Given a choice between running water or water that's still
A dog will drink from the fountain until he gets his fill
There's just something tantalizing about water that moves
It's a great mystery as to why it so attracts, why it soothes

We have very little rain here in this desert clime
We're blessed with sunshine nearly all of the time
And when it rains, it's usually a torrential downpour
Accompanied by thunder and lightning—a lion's roar

But this week, I was able to take a walk in a gentle rain
It reminded me of Fred Astaire's happy, sloshing refrain
Dancing and splashing about with umbrella in hand
Expressing a joy that only a child seems to understand

But as I walked with the rain softly floating down
It was as if the running water had silenced all sound
Not only that, but all my cares vanished into thin air
And I could sense nature's revival everywhere

The smoky clouds made it seem like the mountain was on fire
One could not help but pause and, for just a minute, admire
An amazing scene that only God could put together
Somehow, the rain just seemed to make everything better

This fast-paced world isn't one to provide solace
To realize the peace God so clearly promised
But when it rains again in a slow, drizzling way
I'll be in my raincoat, and the walk will make my day

I'm sure many of you might think I am totally nuts
After all, isn't this weather why God made ducks?
But before you laugh and hold me in utter disdain
Put away your doubts and take a walk in the rain.

Every Life Needs a Little Sugar

Americans have been getting fatter for a long time
Sugar has taken the blame for our expanding waistline
And carbohydrates are the kissing cousins as well
Because they break down to glucose to fuel our cells

I see people walking away from sugar like it's a toxin
Consuming even the smallest amount almost a sin
But we can't live our lives based solely on vinegar
I'm convinced every life needs a little sugar

What would life be without a little sugar in our bloodstream?
Cake, cookies, snickers, and an occasional bowl of ice cream
Leave behind that boring diet of tofu and meat
And kick it up a notch or two with something sweet

Sugar is also a great metaphor for how we are to live
A little sweetness toward others and quick to forgive
Sow a little kindness, joy, and love wherever you are
And you'll light up a somber room like a rock star

As a little sugar will add zest to many a recipe
Your grace is the spiritual sugar of life's rhapsody
Compassion and sensitivity are also quite sugary
And they'll spur those around you to renewed vitality

So you see, sugar has gotten a bad rap all along
It's the sauce of life that picks us up like a favorite song
When you see someone who's struggling, down and out
Hit them with a little sugar and watch the turnabout.

FIND YOUR PUDDLE

I'm always intrigued by how a dog reacts to a puddle
You can bet his actions are anything but subtle
Most likely, he'll go prancing through the little lake
Exiting all wet and frisky, make no mistake

Whereas people would just stop and walk around
The dog runs through the middle in a few bounds
He just seems to find so much joy in this little escapade
Romping in sheer delight, a new game to be played

Kids will react to a puddle in much the same way
Boots or not, the puddle is an invitation to play
And the joy they find is written all over their faces
Giggling and splashing through the deepest places

So what puddles do we have that wildly exhilarate?
What elevates our joy and raises our heart rate?
What makes us forget our troubles for just a bit
Or makes us laugh till we just can't quit?

Maybe your puddle is the adrenalin of a skydiving trip
Or the adventure of crewing a sailing ship
Maybe it's a dive to the darkest depths of the sea
Or the beauty of a cruise through the isles of Hawaii

Maybe it's a hike down the Grand Canyon one time
Or a dinner cruise down the River Rhine
Maybe it's joining your kids on the slip-and-slide
Something bringing joy you just can't hide

Maybe it's a trip to Africa you thought could never be
Seeing the animals up close, roaming wild and free
Or building a snowman together after a heavy snow
Or whisking down a scary zip line in old Mexico

Jesus said, "I come that you would have life to the full"
Our lives were never meant to be just a daily struggle
Joy in heaven, yes, but we also need it on Earth
Each day we should be living it for all it's worth

There's a puddle out there, just waiting for you
It's a puddle that only you can run through
Life is too short to have it be just a muddle
But it's up to you to find your puddle.

FREE

What does it mean to be truly free?
Here's a picture that may explain it adequately
Let go of your dog's leash with the gate open wide
In a few seconds, he'll vanish from your side

He's running free to somewhere he's never been
You don't know if he'll come back or when
His ears are flopping, and he's off to parts unknown
And only when he's hungry will he return home

Remember the end of the school year, summer vacation?
Running from the building in total celebration
Or when you finally graduated to life's next phase
Throwing your cap in the air in freedom's craze

How about that day when you could finally drive?
Out on the road, feeling blessed just to be alive
It's a sense of freedom like none other, unsurpassed
A sense of controlling your own destiny at last

Then there's the freedom of retirement come due
When you can finally discover the hidden you
When Monday mornings never again matter
And talk of deadlines is just so much chatter

Ask someone who's lived in a totalitarian regime
If freedom doesn't qualify as a blessed dream
Ask them what they'd give up to be totally free
And you'll find no limits to the value of liberty

Many of our soldiers paid an unbelievable price
Most of us cannot imagine the extent of their sacrifice
They risked their life without hesitation or thought
And the world is envious of the freedom they bought

But these freedoms pale in comparison to this one
The day you accepted Jesus as God's only Son
When you felt like you really were born again
Freeing you forever from the power of sin

It's the day you finally knew the meaning of truth
It was not the answer to what but the answer to who
Jesus said the way, the truth, and the life is Me
You will know the truth, and the truth will set you free

And that, my friends, is the greatest freedom of all
Placing your trust in the Lord when you hear Him call
You'll feel like someone gave you the Fort Knox key
And you'll know for the first time the true meaning of free.

LIKE A CHILD

Innocent, trusting, excited over little things
A song in their heart they're willing to sing
Humble and awed by what they don't understand
Impossible challenge; they still think they can

They are wide-eyed and inquisitive right from the start
Bringing unquestioning faith and a joyful heart
They've not been cynicized by the world's concerns
Have an unequaled capacity to experience and learn

They respect authority, with only a few excursions
To mother and father, they are more joy than burden
They show us that laughter absolutely is the best medicine
And we never tire of watching their daily shenanigans

They run to father or mother when they skin their knees
And what parent can resist requests that begin with "please"?
They go through their days seemingly without worry or care
Knowing their parents, their protectors will always be there

Time has no relevance to the things they like to do
And they respond immediately to praise and "I love you"
Their minds are unencumbered with worry and fret
They run free as a deer, and setbacks quickly forget

We all know who it is that steals our heart and makes us smile
And pleases the Father with their innocence all the while
Jesus said, "You must become like a child to be with Me"
Come with a heart that's pure and a spirit that's free

The Lord is also waiting for you with love and open arms
He's there to protect you from any disaster or harm
All you have to do is ask for forgiveness and freedom from sin
And He'll be there to welcome you as you run to Him

We, the adults, are supposed to be the teachers of Christ
But children often teach us more of what it means to be nice
So if you're drifting from the Lord and things are a little wild
Step up your humility, simplify, and come to Him like a child.

LOOK FOR THE CIRRUS

Whether we care to admit it or not, our moods change
And the changes often cannot be explained
One day we're soaring high and going with the flow
And the next day, we're about as low as we can go

Anytime you're in serious need of some inspiration
Just look around at the many wonders of God's creation
Rainbows, mountains, flowers, and babbling brook
They're all there to marvel at if you just take a look

One of the many visual blessings of our amazing God
Are the many kinds of clouds there for us to be awed
As a kid, and even now, they stimulate my imagination
Bringing forth a moment of complete captivation

One would look like a castle, another like a fort or a bear
Maybe it was a lion, a warrior, or a pirate ship up there
For each one, I might see the picture, and you would not
You would see something else, a totally different thought

The clouds may put on their show in a multitude of ways
Their display as varied as there are stars or the year has days
And each may have something to do with our mood
Creating either a tendency to smile or sullenly brood

Nimbus clouds are the dark ones we associate with fear
They often come with lightning and the thunder we hear
But they also bring to the plants and animals blessed rain
And its power and might remind us that God still reigns

The stratus clouds are like a blanket, an impenetrable sheet
It's like a door closing, making the loss of view complete
Because these clouds are often very low in the sky
Our glass may seem half full, and we don't know why

Cumulus clouds are white, fluffy, a little like cotton balls
Our interest in naming their shapes is what so enthralls
We are not limited in any way in our ability to imagine
And, in the process, whisked to a place we've never been

But my favorite of all are the cirrus which look like a feather
They stretch across the sky, whimsical but banded together
Their finger-like projections seem to softly touch each other
They're connected like family or lover to lover

The cirrus are the happy clouds that elevate our mood
They're the peace and contentment our souls have pursued
There to remind us of all the blessings God has bestowed
To lift us from our worries, to smile, and to lighten our load

So when life is so difficult that you just want to give up
I pray for cirrus clouds to lift your spirit; overflow your cup
Life is often full of trouble, and we need something to cheer us
So just raise your eyes to the heavens and look for the cirrus.

LOOK UP

"Look down, look down," sings prisoner, Jean Valjean
A sad refrain with all sense of dignity gone
And he continues, "Don't look 'em in the eye"
In *Les Miserables*, it's his heart-wrenching cry

The Bible says, to the mountains I lift my eyes
From whence comes my help; my hopes rise
There's no help coming from below the ground
So why not look up instead of looking down?

But then we all seem to be lowering our gaze
And it begins at even the earliest of age
Discipline a child and watch as his head drops
Looking down is indicative of just being distraught

We carry this on, this lowering of our sights
And it doesn't matter if it's day or night
There are people we encounter on the streets
But with heads down, they're ones we'll never meet

As we age, the problem becomes even worse
It just seems to be the octogenarian's curse
We watch our steps carefully, not to fall down
And we look at our feet as we shuffle around

Technology has added fuel to this downward glance
We work the iPads and iPhones as if in a trance
Even at dinner, sometimes we just work those thumbs
Have we improved even a bit when all this surfing is done?

But on those rare occasions when our head's lifted
We can savor some of the sights our God gifted
Allow yourself to be mesmerized by golden sunsets
And snow-crested mountains are as good as it gets

Clouds of all kinds will paint the daytime art
And the nighttime stars will warm your heart
The moon's glow will add its own bit of charm
You'll feel optimism that deflects all harm

When someone needs help, they always look to the sky
With hands raised, they'll not look down, and here's why
The God of the Universe is waiting there to lessen their burden
When they look up to Him in prayer, it's virtually certain

Remember your earthly father coming home from someplace?
You had to look up to see the happiness on his face
And it brought you a joy it was impossible to hide
Look up; your Heavenly Father waits with arms open wide

So why go around with your attitude down and out?
Look up, child, and discover what living is all about
Make a change in your life; hop out of that rut
Your whole world will be better if you just look up

I believe God communicates in many different ways
That there are no coincidences filling out our days
I'm sitting at the coffee shop, sipping from my cup
And above my head is an ad that starts with "look up"

So I'm going to make a real effort to raise my head
Not casting my eyes down but looking up instead
It will be a demonstration of everything that I believe
And I know my God in heaven will be absolutely pleased.

SHIMMER BY THE LIGHT OF THE LORD

I love to sit on our patio, gazing at our fountain
It's on a par with looking at our magnificent mountains
There's something about the sight and sound of running water
That seems to take away the stress any day has authored

I can appreciate the fountain's serenity any time of day
But sunset brings out its beauty like a New York ballet
I can sit there and be enveloped by its mesmerizing sound
Water bubbling up and, just as quickly, cascading down

Sunset is an amazing addition to this spectacle, though
As light hits the fountain, the water shimmers and adds to the show
The shimmer and glimmer draw attention for all to see
The mind drifts to a time when life was easier and carefree

You can see the same shimmer on an afternoon lake
It's an effect that only water, light, and God can make
So it is as well with the meandering river or babbling brook
And to feel its peace, all you have to do is pause and look

I wonder if I shimmer when God shines His light on me
And when people look, I wonder what person they see
Do I present a picture of peace and attract them to Christ
Or do I lose the glitter of His love and amazing sacrifice

God can turn any ordinary person into one displaying His glory
You can be a reflection of Him by simply telling your story
No matter that you're not perfect and still a sinner
People will pay attention—in His light, you shimmer

Some may not even notice you and just pass on by
But if you're shimmering, they'll stop, not understanding why
They'll know there's a reason it's you they're drawn toward
And one day, they'll know you shimmer by the light of the Lord.

SILENCE

Psalm 46:10 tells us to be still and know
I'm the God of the Universe; I'm in control
Only by shutting out the world and being still
Do we have a chance to understand His will

Mother Teresa said it best "God is the friend of silence;
He cannot be found in noise and restlessness;
See how the trees, flowers, and grass grow in quiet;
Silently the stars, moon, and sun move compliant"

"The heavens declare the glory of God," says Psalm 19:1
His glory is also found on Earth, displaying what He has done
The beauty of nature rings quietly without compare
The mountains, the valleys, and the flowers that grow there

The forest provides the perfect venue where peace reigns
In the silence, allow God to take control of your heart and brain
It will be subtle—that's the way God touches our soul
But in the quiet, you may realize it's Him who's in control

Sit there in the woods and just listen in wonderment for awhile
Hear the wind whistling through the trees, off a mile
The leaves, with their shaking, may be God speaking to you
Just like at Pentecost when the Holy Spirit blew through

It will be unmistakable and clear; you'll feel His presence
In the solitude, you'll be touched by a sense of reverence
Don't pass it off that what I'm feeling is all in my mind
Savor the moment with Him; this is what God designed

When you return to the clamor and noise of the everyday
Learn to relish those moments listening to what God has to say
Find that place like the deep forest where noise is set aside
And where you and your Lord can communicate side by side.

SLOWLY I TURN

You've heard how Dr. Doolittle talked to the animals, I trust
But did you know how God created each one to speak to us?
The animal kingdom exhibits an amazing array
Of messages delivered to us in their own special way

For example, let's look at the lion, one without apprehension
When he opens his mouth to roar, all pay attention
The word that comes to mind for me is "bold"
We're to be fearless in our testimony, young or old

How about the coyote, the one who travels in packs
What they can do together is what one alone lacks
I think the word I associate with them is "together"
Working as a team always yields results that are better

One of the most intriguing creatures is the hummingbird
It's so easy to characterize them with just the right word
Tiny, but they do things no others can do; they're "unique"
We have strengths like no other as well, even if we're meek

The eagle can soar to the highest heights with ease
Able to "ballet" in the strongest gale or the slightest breeze
The word he embodies is quite clearly "majesty"
When we worship the Lord, that's what we should see

Let's consider an animal a little closer to home, the dog
In this case, the word is extremely easy to catalog
Everything your dog does comes with a helping of "love"
A word prominent in the commandments sent from above

Here's an animal in the kingdom that might make you scoff
But don't rush to judgment before I tell you about the sloth
He has facial muscles that seem to create a permanent smile
And wouldn't that be a good thing for us all the while?

The sloth lives in trees, high above the worldly fray
What goes on down on the jungle floor is mostly bad anyway
Worrying about things out of your control has no use
Be like the sloth who 95 percent of the time just hangs loose

The sloth is the slowest-moving mammal under the sun
He's probably the only animal in the kingdom you'll never see run
His glacial pace is laughable but does much to conserve energy
His keen sense of smell and recall make up for his lethargy

Can you imagine the scene when Noah was loading the ark?
With all the other animals on board and it getting dark
Finally, the sloths appear on the ramp as the rain begins to fall
God's waiting, but there's only one gear in their crawl

When I think of the sloth, slow and methodical come to mind
Something to emulate, never in a hurry, never short of time
The word "patience" seems to characterize his major attribute
And saying we could use some of that is absolute truth

We're never going to slow down to the sloth's sluggish pace
But maybe we'll slow down just enough to leave the rat race
And when we do, maybe we'll understand the sloth's worth
And why God smiled when He placed him here on Earth

So you see, the animals speak to us through what they do
We should pay attention; with each activity, they send us clues
We can learn a lot by watching them, just being still
Using their examples to behave according to God's will.

THAT ORDINARY YOU

The night was ordinary in every way
The dark overcame the light in the usual way
Maybe there was a gust of wind somewhere
Or maybe there was a hint of chill in the air

Maybe it was a beautiful night in December
But it wasn't one likely you'd remember
Not one of surprise to keep you awake
No fiery red sunset over a peaceful lake

The sheep were on the hillside, bedded down
Most eyes closed, not making a sound
Just lumps in the night, silhouettes
Loved as a master would love his pets

The shepherds were there, destitute and poor
None of their clothes bought at a department store
They were a simple and nameless lot
Knowledgeable and worldly, they were not

Ordinary night, ordinary shepherds, ordinary sheep
Nothing you'd write in your journal to keep
Were it not for the Lord, this night would pass
Without anything to remember or anything to last

But the Lord deals every day with the ordinary
And His hand quickly transforms it to extraordinary
The common becomes uncommon for a reason
And 2000 years later, we celebrate the season

Suddenly, the sky explodes; shepherds on their feet
Sheep, once content, are a chorus of bleat
The night would be ordinary no more
His Son had come to Earth as prophesied before

That's God's workplace—simple, ordinary, and weak
The ones who need Him most are the ones He seeks
All of our limitations, our imperfections, and sins
That's where the power of the Lord begins

So, if you'll just bring Him your ordinary stuff
His awesome strength and love are more than enough
To transform your life, make it exciting and new
And you won't recognize that ordinary you.

WASTING TIME

Don't we just love being busy all the time?
Filling up our senses with almost anything we can find
And the digital world we're in is a willing accomplice
Assuring that nothing gets by us, there's nothing we miss

During our careers, our importance may have hinged on busyness
Societal pressures suggesting we couldn't take time to just rest
Even in retirement, it seems there's very little quiet time
Volunteering, socializing, and chores contribute to the daily grind

Otis Redding was famous for his song, "The Dock of the Bay"
"I'm sittin' on the dock of the bay, watchin' the tide roll away,
Sittin' on the dock of the bay, wasting time"
He makes the thought of just sitting there seem perfectly fine

I love the idea of wasting time, doing nothing but sitting
And doing so next to the ocean would seem perfectly fitting
There's something mesmerizing and calming with nothing to do
And if it's accompanied by an ocean breeze, mood-lifting too

While you sit, you'll find thoughts running through your head
Maybe you'll contemplate the meaning of some book you read
Maybe you'll just marvel at the world God created
Taking the time to look around and be totally captivated

Maybe your "bay" is a mountaintop or a nature preserve
Some place where "wasting time" can be reserved
You'll find it soul-satisfying, attitude-changing, and healing
Time to walk from the chaos and get in touch with your feelings

Society tends to look down on the idea of wasting time
But give it a chance, and I think here's what you'll find
God is waiting for you to wait for Him on the bay
Rest there awhile and watch the tide roll in and away

God loves to speak to us when our hearts and minds are clear
And the conversation will be with love and forgiveness, not fear
So when the world is pulling you down, and you're out on a limb
You can sit on the dock, waste time, and turn it all over to Him.

PERSEVERANCE—FELLOWSHIP

"Not only so, but we also glory in our sufferings, because we know that suffering produces perseverance; perseverance, character; and character, hope"
(Romans 5:3–4, NIV).

"As iron sharpens iron, so one person sharpens another"
(Proverbs 27:17, NIV).

Allegory of the Mountain

There were five men who surveyed a mountain to climb
Physically they were the same, but not of the same mind
Their stated goal was to persevere all the way to the top
But not all would make the summit before deciding to stop

There were four scenic viewpoints provided all along the way
At each, some of God's most beautiful creations were on display
At the base, freedom was met by the boundaries of the worldview
Limited perspective, bias, and transgressions, more than a few

But for some unknown reason, one just couldn't leave it
If there was something better higher up, he couldn't see it
Only four continued on to viewpoint one at 3000 feet
And discovered that at the base, the view was incomplete

Now they could see the valley was wider and longer than before
The vista created a much greater expanse for the eyes to explore
Happy with what he was seeing, one man decided that was enough
Climbing to the next level was going to be too arduous and tough

So three men pushed on from there to the stop at 6000 feet
And acknowledged the view from there just couldn't be beat
They could now see all of the nearby city and county land
Things that never made sense before they could now understand

But it had been a challenging climb to reach this next level
And the third man quit, inspired by the incentive killer, the devil
So now there were only two who pushed on to 9000 feet
Beginning to feel the effects of altitude as they took a seat

Now they were treated to a view of the whole state below
Saw the beauty of the forests, lakes, and the first hint of snow
One of them was content with what he had seen and learned
And couldn't resist the call of the valley, beckoning for his return

And so, of the five, only one hung in there and reached the summit
There had been plenty of trials and tribulations, but he had overcome it
And his reward was a view that the others could only imagine, never see
It stretched for miles, the Creator's painting of Earth in all its majesty

Somehow, up here, the truth seemed much easier to find
All the lies, distortions, and half-truths left behind
In the quiet solitude, there was the blessing of freedom at last
As night separates from day, a remarkable and startling contrast

The air was as clean and as invigorating as freshly fallen snow
He felt sad that the others would never experience it, never know
What it was like to witness all the glory the Maker had to give
And that perched on the mountaintop was the only way to live.

GOD'S FINISH LINE

If you were a marathon runner, I think you'll relate
Even if your success was a tad short of great
Learnings from that experience are still applicable today
In responding to life's challenges thrown your way

First and foremost, in running, you must have a plan
You can't sprint the whole way even if you think you can
You must conserve energy for the inevitable hills
And save a kick for the end when you're short on will

In every race ever run, your body, at some point, wants to quit
Bring an end to the pain, give it up, and be done with it
But there's a voice inside that tells you to press on
Just take a few more strides, and the victory can be won

I think there's an analogy here about our run for Christ
What are we willing to give up, what to sacrifice?
When the body is weak, will the spirit overcome?
Will we be able to kick it in and finish the run?

The difference between the distance runner and life's grind
Is that, in life, we cannot see how far it is to the finish line
How can we be assured that we've run our best race
If we don't know the distance and don't set the right pace

But then comes the Helper who's always by our side
The Invisible One in whom we can trust and truly confide
The Holy Spirit is there to share with us God's plan
Bringing the example of Jesus to every woman and man

Like the distance runner, we're to be in it for the long haul
Running the race God set out for us, pleasing Him above all
We will stumble at times when rough road comes into play
But Jesus will be waiting with open arms at the end of our days

We will tire, and every muscle in our body will tell us to quit
But then we think about the cross, and we'll have none of it
Like the runner, we push on, persevering over body and mind
And finally, in glory, stretch out over God's finish line.

Good and Faithful Servant—Well Done

He came into the world in the usual way
But was forced to lay His head on a blanket of hay
Only a select few knew this was the King
Or that one day He'd be the Master of everything

His childhood was no indication of what was to come
Or what impact He'd have when His work was done
He challenged the establishment right from the start
Spoke with authority words directly from the heart

Twelve ordinary men became His followers, His band
Carrying a message even they didn't understand
He was a peasant, humble, but committed to His course
His power just seemed to come from a different source

His followers grew in number each and every day
The establishment became very concerned about the Way
Time and time again, they failed to prove Him a fraud
This man might be, as He claimed, the Son of God

He was a threat to all the power they held dear
They had to eliminate Him; that much was clear
Trumped-up charges were at the heart of this scam
They just didn't know they were part of His plan

But, with a mob mentality, they sent Him to the cross
Even His most ardent followers thought His life a loss
He seemed ordinary when He called to His Father out loud
When the atonement was complete, and His head was bowed

But the hope was rekindled when He arose from the grave
And they knew it was only through Him they could be saved
That eternity wasn't just a nice thought to sugarcoat death
That the last air on Earth wasn't to be their last breath

The Holy Spirit Jesus had promised came at Pentecost
And ordinary men proclaimed His message at extreme cost
All suffered incredible punishment, and most died a horrible death
Yet they stood by their Lord and Savior till their last breath

Most of us will not suffer this kind of anguish in our testimony
But we will be challenged with persecution and acrimony
Like the twelve, when that happens, we must stand tall
Keeping Christ in view and following the example of Paul

And when our work here on Earth has come to an end
And it is time for us to follow our Lord; to heaven ascend
I pray that He would be there to start us on our eternal run
With this greeting, "Oh, good and faithful servant, well done!"

GROWING IN THE VALLEY

Life is often characterized as a series of valleys and hills
Valleys are the downers bringing life's unwanted ills
The hills or mountains are times when we're riding high
It's a walk on easy street, and there's no reason to cry

It's in the valley where the challenges reside
Where there's nowhere to run, no place to hide
We have to stand, find the fortitude to push through
And in so doing, find that strength we never knew

Did you ever notice nothing grows on the highest peak?
Blinding snow and numbing cold paint a picture bleak
But it's in the valley where plants blossom and grow
Overcoming torrential rains or destructive winds that blow

Our lives are not the guy-gets-the-girl movie from Hollywood
Where we find it easy to rejoice and times are good
There is suffering, trauma, sickness, and loss
And healing only comes at the base of the cross

Jesus never said life would be a walk in the park
But for every challenge, there is a strengthening of the heart
He told us to rejoice in our suffering, never mope
For it will lead to perseverance, character-building, and hope

The Lord never promised to take us around the storms that brew
But rather that He would be with us to guide us through
Like the rain that causes the plants to grow stronger and more beautiful
We are better and of greater service for being purified in the crucible

I'm sure it would be great if we could spend our life on the heights
Where there was not a moment of panic, and we bathed in starry nights
But our witness for Christ is stronger when we overcome
Grow in character and finish the race to be run.

Growth Is Fueled by a Lifetime of Mistakes

When we look back, it's easy to see we all made mistakes
But unlike Hollywood, it's usually impossible to do retakes
And all of them come with a measure of sorrow and regret
It can become difficult to move on, change, and forget

In those cases where we can correct what we did wrong
It behooves us to make restitution, not waiting too long
The path to forgiveness may be difficult, but it cleanses the soul
It will quiet that voice you can't seem to control

I think mistakes are a vital part of God's learning curve
How we move from narcissism to a willingness to serve
The God of the Universe gave us the perfect blueprint
Following the example provided through the Son He sent

God is the master potter, and we are just the clay
He molds and makes us according to His will every day
Sometimes our clay is so bad He has to scrap the whole jar
Remaking what we're called to do and who we are

Lest we think our shortcomings are somehow unique
Even icons of the Bible had moments they were weak
Disobedience kept Moses from entering the Promised Land
And David let his attraction to Bathsheba get out of hand

Mistakes often lead to suffering and being unable to cope
But the Bible says suffering leads to character and hope
God is able to use those moments we decide to disobey
Consequences provide strength for whatever's coming our way

A life without mistakes would be wonderful to achieve
But sin entered our lives long ago with Adam and Eve
Mistakes, even bad ones, come with a positive, though
God can take our biggest misstep and use it to help us grow

We are all people completely and seriously flawed
Sometimes stumbling along on our way closer to God
Working to get better every day is the recipe it takes
Knowing that growth is fueled by a lifetime of mistakes.

HEEDING THE CALL

In the movie, *The Lion King*, Simba is the chosen one
He cannot run away from his destiny, who he's to become
Initially, he takes the easy path, escaping to a foreign land
Only after much soul-searching does he begin to understand

He knows he must return to take his rightful place
The challenge will be difficult, but one he must face
His father is there in the quiet to encourage him on
And applauds from afar the renewed character of his son

Simba returns to his homeland to do what he was called to do
It's a task he takes on not just for himself but for others too
And when all is said and done, he follows his father's legacy
Taking up the mantle of leadership and claiming his destiny

Aren't we a little bit like Simba, wanting to run away
When things get more difficult than we can face each day?
When we just can't seem to clear failure from our mind
The mountain before us just seems too imposing to climb

But then there's the call from our Father, the heavenly one
And He reminds us of the sacrifice of His only Son
He tells us all the strength we need will come from Him
Just be bold and obedient, and He'll carry us to a win

And so we step into our destiny, never looking back
With God at our side, finding the courage we once lacked
And as we tackle our fears to claim the brass ring
We'll forever have a bond to the story of *The Lion King*.

IRON SHARPENS IRON

No man is an island, says poet John Dunne
We cannot really live unless we have someone
Man does not live on bread alone
Others into life's tapestry must be sewn

Left to solitary, life brings but misery
We may be free, but there's no liberty
Reading may bless us with some learning
But sharing of ideas keeps our soul burning

We're a social animal, needing community
Anxious to engage others at every opportunity
A table for one is a lonely and depressing sight
A life without fellowship is dark as night

I think Solomon says it best in Proverbs 27
Iron sharpens iron is an important lesson
No one knows everything; only God does
And those knowing nothing never was

We can all learn immeasurably from each other
Whether of the same or another color
We come together with different perspectives
And even long-held positions may be affected

We're better for having been sharpened in wit
Gaining wisdom from others bit by bit
Benefitting from what others have to say
And using that knowledge for the rest of our days

The Lord recognized early on that Adam needed Eve
And believers need others who also believe
The world would have us doubt our faith otherwise
But iron on iron strengthens us against all the lies

It's true; we can accomplish much on our own
But there are limits to achievements alone
God built group dynamics deep into our DNA
Knowing that iron sharpens iron, there's no other way.

SKIP ANOTHER STONE

Have you ever stood by a river, flat stone in hand
And tried to skip it across all the water to dry land?
It takes not only a good throw but a perfect stone
To skip that rock multiple times until it reaches home

Did you ever notice that you fail more times than succeed?
Most times, the rock just falls to the bottom among the weeds
But then, when least expected, a rock skips safely to the other side
And you celebrate with a joy you just cannot hide

You can't throw the stone like a pitcher in baseball
You have to release it sidearm, and that's not all
It involves bending at the waist and a flip of the wrist
Athleticism, yes, but not the skill of a perfectionist

Isn't this a great metaphor for the challenges we face?
We're going to fail more times than we win the race
But once in a while, our "stone" hydroplanes across the river
And with God, we bask in the glory of "stand and deliver"

And we don't have to be perfect in the way things are done
With less than perfect form, the race can still be won
Find a great idea and, with enthusiasm, pitch it across
Even if it falls to the bottom, all is not lost

Look around and find a better idea, a better stone
One that will skip and skip until it reaches home
You'll never know if it will reach the opposite shore
Unless you pick up another and give it a go once more

Some of the most successful people failed multiple times
But they knew the value of persistence of body and mind
And knew that, eventually, they'd bring it all home
By not being afraid to just skip another stone.

SNOWFLAKE

To appreciate the beauty of a snowflake, you have to stand in the cold
Words from Aristotle that shine as precious as gold
Every situation that rewards comes with a sacrifice
Anything worthwhile in life requires paying the price

Accomplishing anything of worth can only be done by immersion
Years of commitment to learning produces the best surgeon
The hall-of-fame quarterback wasn't born that way
Diet, body-building, and practice made him better each day

We didn't learn to be parents by reading some guru's book
Trial and error, mistakes made, and correction are what it took
We don't live according to God's Word; we never start
If we don't read each verse carefully and take it to heart

Love one another is a nice catchphrase we often hear
But without empathy and action, it's just a sideline cheer
To be filled with the Spirit, you must devote time to "The Book"
To really appreciate nature, you have to do more than just look

To learn anything new, you must invest energy and time
Just reading the labels won't make you a connoisseur of wine
Friendships are not made with just a strong handshake
And swimmers are not made by standing at the edge of the lake

World-class athletes improve their skills through hours of practice
Just reading your lines won't make you a revered actress
The comedian spends years building up his successful repertoire
The most comprehensive manual won't teach you to drive a car

The best magicians know there's more to entertaining than sleight of hand
A college degree is important, but it's out in the world you understand
And to get to heaven, you must humble yourself and fall at Jesus' feet
Only then will you be reconciled and your time on Earth complete

You cannot say you're a Christian unless your actions say the same
And under no circumstances would you take His name in vain
The road to God's favor is narrow, but it sparkles like gold
And like the snowflake, its beauty is worth standing in the cold.

THE REDWOOD TREE

Have you ever stood next to a giant redwood tree
And, at that moment, marveled at God's creativity?
Some of them so old they go back to when Christ was on Earth
Displaying heights of 300 feet and a twenty-foot girth

Many have witnessed every catastrophe yet persevered through it all
Neither wind nor rain nor fire could bring about their fall
Their twelve-inch layer of bark offers a natural resistance to insect activity
All of this contributing to an amazing example of longevity

Doesn't the redwood's defense parallel what the Bible has to say
About putting on the armor of God each and every day?
Where the redwood has fashioned an impenetrable layer of bark
The Christian relies on the breastplate of righteousness against the dark

The redwood, for all its height, has a root system not deep
No anchoring tap root, just surface roots extending for 80 feet
Their roots reach out and intertwine with those of trees nearby
And that support gives them a firm foundation to keep them alive

As their interconnected root system keeps the redwood standing tall
So too, as Christians, we need others if we're to answer the call
Fellowship is as important an ingredient as worship and prayer
We can stand tall knowing our brothers will always be there

So you see, the redwood God created is a symbol of us at our best
Bold, standing tall, and persevering against Satan's tests
So, the next time you're challenged, think of the redwood tree
And that image will help you become all God wanted you to be.

WILDFLOWER

The seed finds its resting place where it can
Carried there by animal, wind, or man
It might find fertile soil or only rock
Obligated, though, to wait in dry dock

Then one day, the rains come pouring down
The transformation begins below the ground
Seedling pokes through at the appointed hour
And in all its glory bursts forth the wildflower

One is followed by two; then, quickly, a score
In short order, they fill an acre or more
Red, golden, and blue compose the scheme
We stand in awe, marveling at the scene

Christians are formed in much the same way
A seed is planted by someone one day
It may or may not find a receptive soul
A hardened heart cannot accept the role

Then one day, lightning strikes a spiritual cord
Maybe the right person or just the right word
Maybe it's a tragedy or a friend's advice
That sprouts a new believer in Christ

Unsure of his faith, just a fledgling at first
But strengthened by God and Bible verse
The Holy Spirit comes, and the growth's complete
Like the wildflower, an aroma pure and sweet

But that's only the beginning of this odyssey
Disciple follows disciple in this new ministry
The brothers meet often to fellowship and pray
And strengthen each other in following the Way

Their numbers grow daily as others want to be
With the Lord, as He promised, for all eternity
And when the Lord looks down from His heavenly tower
It's more pleasing to Him than any wildflower.

TRUTH—WORLDVIEW

"Jesus answered, 'You say that I am a king. In fact, the reason I was born and came into the world is to testify to the truth. Everyone on the side of truth listens to me" (John 18:37, NIV).

"Jesus answered, 'I am the way and the truth and the life. No one comes to the Father except through me" (John 14:6, NIV).

"Put to death, therefore, whatever belongs to your earthly nature: sexual immorality, impurity, lust, evil desires and greed, which is idolatry" (Colossians 3:5, NIV).

A Glorious Future Is about to Bloom

Sixty million abortions have been performed under Roe vs. Wade
That's 1.3 million babies every year we've betrayed
They had no voice at all in this decision to end their life
It's murder just as surely as if they were stabbed with a knife

Mass shootings over the last 7 years have totaled 934
From the hysteria, it just seems like there were many more
Not that nothing should be done about these senseless crimes
But for the unborn who were slain, where's the outrage in kind?

Roughly 5 million U. S. soldiers were killed in modern-day wars
For sure, their numbers and sacrifice are hard to ignore
But it still pales in comparison to those who never had a chance
To experience all there is to life—to learn, grow, and advance

Many have rallied around the theme, "Black Lives Matter"
In the news and on the internet, it's created a lot of chatter
There can be no doubt that this catchphrase is certainly true
But shouldn't "Unborn Lives Matter" also be given its due?

Which one might have been the next Newton or Einstein?
Maybe another Lincoln or Martin Luther King we'd find
Which one might have been a player on the world stage
Or won the Nobel Peace Prize before the end of his days?

We'll never know because they never had a chance to speak
It was inconvenient, or maybe our values were just too weak
Why do we find it easier to play God and squelch this voice
Rather than accepting responsibility with a much better choice

One of the key issues seems to be when is life's inception?
Is it at birth, at the first heartbeat, or at conception?
The Lord said, "Before I formed you in the womb I knew you"
I think that proclamation leaves little to misconstrue

Some say, when it comes to her body, it's a woman's right
To decide if the fetus she's carrying will ever see the light
No consideration is given to the right of the baby to find his place
To live, raise a family, or contribute to the human race

When God looks down on how we justify killing the unborn
I believe He reacts with an equal measure of tears and scorn
The time is coming when we'll regret not reaching higher
We'll stand before the throne and face the Lake of Fire

Many women have, after the fact, had second thoughts
As they dealt with the pain, loss, and guilt it brought
Wondering who their child might have turned out to be
And what part he may have played in changing history

I have a personal stake in this drama, as do many others
You see, my birth was the decision of an unwed mother
She just couldn't bring herself to throw me away
Without her choice, I'd not be writing poetry today

For anyone who might be facing this difficult choice
Listen to your heart and the counsel of your inner voice
That's the Lord speaking for the fetus in your womb
Telling you what a glorious future is about to bloom.

BLACK CAN NEVER BE WHITE

When I was a kid, the bad guys always wore black
And they always lost to those in white; that's a fact
We cheered on the good guys, knowing they were right
Things might look bad, but they always won the fight

It was a simpler time with very little gray
Completely the opposite of what we have today
The words in the Bible made everything crystal clear
If we did wrong, it was the wrath of God we feared

White is the truth; not determined by the beholder's eyes
And black presents itself as a growing pack of lies
The gray happens when it's a half-truth we buy
Despite how close it is to the truth, it's still a lie

Even less noticeable and harder to discern
Is something that every career politician has learned
People will buy my fabrications again and again
If I just tell the story with the proper amount of spin

Accepting half-truths is the start down a slippery slope
In short order, finding the truth has lost all hope
The lies build on one another until there's no end
And we accept them like a long-lost friend

Look at what's happened to our society today
The lies have become so widespread we've lost our way
Pre-marital sex isn't even given a second thought
And killing babies is a right women have fanatically sought

We don't even know if we're women or men
Or which bathroom we're supposed to attend
And apparently, that decision is subject to change
Depending on how our hormones rearrange

The last time the U. S. was debt-free was 1835
The bill today is $92,000 for every person alive
Our politicians lead us to believe we're doing fine
But we all know in our hearts it's just another line.

Thugs are wearing the white hats of individuality
And placing black hats on those in authority
We don't stand for the flag our ancestors died for
Or the ones who are still dying on some distant shore

If we blend black with white, we always get gray
And if we do it long enough, only black will be in play
No matter that some try to convince us this is all right
In our hearts, we know black can never be white.

I Fly

In this age when some choose to denigrate the U. S. flag
And try to make us believe there's more wrong than right
They don't understand the cost of freedom, the price tag
Why our soldiers willingly risk their lives to stand and fight

I wonder if our flag could speak what it would say
Why it waves gloriously over the sea and decorates the sky
Why it moves with the grace of a Baryshnikov ballet
Maybe it would tell us these are the reasons why

I fly for the daring patriots who sent the British home
For those who fought across our land to end slavery
For those in Flanders Fields, honored in a poem
For the soldiers at Normandy and their unequaled bravery

But I also fly for the ordinary men and women of this land
Who know the value of liberty and give it the high ground
Who work hard every day to make a life and understand
Government serves the people, not the other way around

I fly as a beacon of hope for a world downtrodden and poor
Who look to the United States as an opportunity for a new start
Who risk their health and security to come knocking at our door
Knowing there is something better of which they can be a part

I've been set on fire, stamped into the ground, and disgraced
But I still fly every day for those who honor my legacy
Those who still believe God is there dispensing His grace
And for those who sacrificed it all on distant shores for thee

So when you are asked to stand and place your hand on heart
Do it willingly; stand tall as the banner waves through the sky
Think of how blessed you are to live here and do your part
To tell others how important it is to honor the reasons I fly.

SHED THE SHACKLES

I'm sure you're familiar with Plato's *Allegory of the Cave*
Three prisoners shackled to the wall of this dark enclave
Since birth, they've only seen shadows on the opposite wall
Those shadows represent in entirety their knowledge of all

Then one day, one of the prisoners finds a way to break free
He leaves the cave to a truth he could not previously see
At first, he is blinded by the sun, and it's painful to his eyes
Nothing visible through the pain, no matter how hard he tries

He longs to return to the cave where familiarity reigns
A reality he knows; there's comfort in the chains
But he is somehow drawn to the sun and its clarifying appeal
Ever so gradually, his eyes adjust, and new truths are revealed

But once the darkness of the cave has been overcome by the sun
A whole new life of understanding and wisdom has begun
But when the prisoner returns to the cave to tell his friends
They just cannot accept the news or even try to comprehend

They do not understand venturing out of the cave to finally be free
Preferring to spend their lives in chains through all eternity
They even begin plotting how to eliminate the one shining the light
Because they only believe what's on the wall and directly in their sight

Isn't this allegory a lot like Christ coming to Earth to save the lost
Bringing light to a world of darkness and at a terrible cost
His radiance so bright they could not see He was the Truth and the Way
And many are still in the cave of shadows and lost to this day

It's a leap of faith that leads us out of the darkness and into the light
Only the awesome power of the Lord can illuminate the night
So if you're still chained to that wall of darkness, there's hope for thee
Shade your eyes, step into the light; the truth will set you free

Christ came to Earth and took on human form to show us what's true
There's a life outside that dismal cave that's both exciting and new
You'll wonder why it took you so long to end this aberrant behavior
Shed the shackles and heed the calling of your Lord and Savior.

WE ARE NOT

He is Eternal; He is Father
He is The Good Shepherd; He is Glory
He is the Creator of everything we've got
He is Love, and all of these we are not

He is All-Powerful; He is All-Knowing
He is Perfect; He is the Provider
He is the Savior; we've been bought
He is Righteous, and all of these we are not

He is Sovereign; He is The Alpha and Omega
He is Grace; He is the Great I Am
He is Infinite; we're just a dot
He is Holy, and all of these we are not

He is Justice; He is Mercy
He is the Healer; He is The Way
He is Lord, lest we forgot
He is King, and all of these we are not

God said, "Be still, and know that I am God"
We are to worship Him and be awed
He owns us, and He owns our soul
So why do we even think we're in control?

THE GREAT COMMISSION

"Therefore go and make disciples of all nations, baptizing them in the name of the Father and of the Son and of the Holy Spirit" (Matthew 28:19, NIV).

AMBASSADORS FOR CHRIST

Because non-believers are lost
We Christians have a job to do

Because non-believers have a choice
We must make Christ the only choice

Because non-believers can be sensitive
We must respect their feelings

Because non-believers have questions
We must have wisdom

Because non-believers are unique
We must be adaptable

Because non-believers are searching for meaning
We must be responsive

Because non-believers have needs
We must be willing to serve

Because non-believers may be slow to trust
We must be a friend

Because non-believers must understand His sacrifice
We have to be ambassadors for Christ.

IT'S NOT THAT COMPLICATED

Books, books, and more books have been written by theologians on God's Word
The length to which writers will go to help us understand is almost absurd
I once read one and a half pages on the implications of the word "therefore"
Kind of makes you wonder what the unanalyzed Bible is there for

Are there books of the Bible that we need help with to completely digest?
Yes, there are; the book of Revelation is one of them I might suggest
Symbolism that we are unfamiliar with prompts us to ask what and why
Dragons, the four horsemen, strange creatures, and the rolling up of the sky

So what are the tenets of Christianity? What do we believe?
When we are talking to nonbelievers, what story do we weave?
Will they be receptive if we offer endless theology for them to read?
Or do we just give them the gospel, knowing that's all they really need?

God sent His Son to Earth to reconcile mankind to Him
The story goes like this—Jesus took our place and died for our sins
He was buried, and after three days, He was raised from the dead
Five hundred people saw Him alive again, and that's all that needs to be said

He sent the Holy Spirit to give His disciples the power to go forth
And proclaim His message to Judea, Samaria, and all the Earth
The fact that these men were willing to die horrible deaths for this God-Man
Should tell us the strength of their beliefs in taking a stand

Despite all that's been written by experts, it's all there in the Great Book
It's God communicating to us directly if we'll just take time to look
In its simplicity, you'll believe in the resurrection, or you won't
And that will prompt you to worship Him as your Lord, or it won't

So read all the commentaries you want if it helps; read many a book
But while you're doing that, make sure you go back to "The Book"
If you do that, God will make it all clear and reserve your place
It's not that complicated, folks, to accept His amazing grace.

It's You God Wants to Send

A miracle is an event not explicable by natural or scientific law
Those recorded in the Bible leave us with a sense of awe
The feeding of the five thousand and the parting of the Red Sea
Turning water into wine at Cana and Lazarus to vitality

God certainly has the power to turn a miracle at any time
Creation and The Flood—amazing events that come to mind
When all the best minds throw up their hands and call it spiritual
You can be sure that God is at work, bringing forth a miracle

We still acknowledge miracles today when there's no other explanation
And we've eliminated every other alternative from consideration
It's the terminal cancer patient who gets a clean bill of health
The patient in an extended coma who begins to speak for himself

There are other events we'd probably not put in the miracle category
They are amazing but happen without the same measure of glory
It's the unexpected check that hits your mail at just the right time
Conversations with a close friend that shift your personal paradigm

It's the neighbor who brings you a hot meal when you're down and out
The gift that arrives when troubles are more than you can count
The chance encounter with a stranger who makes you laugh
Just when the world has taken your attitude to half staff

If you look at the times when a blessing came through, I think you'll discover
That it wasn't through your own efforts, but the efforts of another
It was God sending someone to lift you up and soothe your distress
Relieving your burden with understanding, empathy, and finesse

This is the way I believe God responds to most of our prayers
It's not generally a miracle performed that shows He cares
It's that quiet voice that whispers in someone's ear
That they are the ones who can make some problem disappear

Sometimes when a friend needs help, it's clear as a bell
At other times God's message doesn't come through nearly as well
But He'll keep reminding us until we finally listen
And take action on someone's desperate condition

I'm sure we can look at numerous times along the way
When a calling brought hope to us for another day
And just when we thought no one really cared
There was God sending someone in answer to our prayer

So be attentive and listen when that voice comes to you
Telling you who's hurting and suggesting what you can do
You won't be able to ignore it, whether stranger or friend
You're not a miracle worker, but it's you God wants to send.

LIGHT UP THE WORLD

Did you ever notice life is full of contrasts?
Things are either moving slow or moving fast
The extremely wealthy and the extremely poor
Those content with less; those who want more

The patient one and the one who can never wait
Arrogant versus humble; love versus hate
The gentle one versus the one in your face
The one laid back; the one at a frenetic pace

The difference between the truth and a white lie
Young or old; the hearty laugh or heartfelt cry
Knowing what's wrong and knowing what's right
There is some gray, but it's mostly black or white

The most dramatic contrast of all is darkness and light
Light rules during the day and darkness at night
But light and darkness aren't just contrasts; they're adversaries
They have nothing in common, no similarities

Have you ever watched how a cockroach behaves?
In the dark, he's doing what he does, unafraid
But turn on the lights, and he zooms to the nearest hole
Staying alive for another day is his only goal

Darkness associates itself with gloom and evil deeds
Light, though, has joy and happiness as its seeds
Darkness provides cover for all manner of despicable acts
And deals in fabrication and half-truths instead of facts

Darkness is the realm of Satan, the evil one
Light is the realm of Jesus Christ, God's only Son
Jesus said I am the light of the earth
Follow Me, and you'll have life for all it's worth

Darkness can prevail as long as there's no light
But even the smallest flicker illuminates the night
Satan has no legitimacy, no rightful place
Standing next to the glorious glow of God's face

We all have a light to shine in the darkness as well
As ambassadors, God had given us quite a story to tell
There are dark corners everywhere for you to mine
So turn on that bright light of yours and let it shine

God will be with you, supplying all the power you need
Walking beside you to help you succeed
And to Him, it will be like finding a precious pearl
You doing your part to light up the world.

Twelve Ordinary Men

They were just twelve ordinary men
Living out their lives in the simplest way
You wouldn't have chosen any of them
Blue collar workers, we'd call them today

Several fishermen, a fanatic, and a tax man
What could we really expect them to do?
Either despised or of no account back then
What they were capable of, no one knew

They had the greatest teacher in the world
But they couldn't grasp the essence of His mission
They listened, but it was as if they never heard
These were not men of great speech or vision

They had intensive training for three years
And yet, at the crucial moment, they were lost
Denying they even knew Him, they gave in to their fears
And watched in horror as their leader died on the cross

But God had yet to unleash His extraordinary power
They had no idea of what was coming; what was in store
The Holy Spirit would be sent at the appointed hour
And their ordinary lives would be ordinary no more

Like a tiny flame quickly becomes a raging fire when given air
These twelve took the Gospel to the ends of the earth
Their Great Commission was no longer one of despair
It was as if they had experienced a second birth

Aren't we like the twelve—just ordinary folk after all
Struggling to make a living; trying to survive
But not really living until we receive the call
And take up a higher reason to be alive

God has a purpose for each of us; a reason, a goal
The power of the Holy Spirit will show us the way
Follow the calling as the twelve did so long ago
And ordinary can still become extraordinary today.

WHERE'S THE MEANING IN LIFE?

I leave the womb, I live, and then I die
But did I ever answer the question why?
What was the purpose of being placed here on Earth?
And am I fulfilling that purpose for all it's worth?

The earth was turning long before my song
And it will continue doing so long after I'm gone
I'm just a grain of sand among a billion others
What is there that's meaningful; what to discover?

The rivers run to the oceans and back again
The way they've been doing for years on end
The earth continues revolving to record the years
The sun sets; then hurries along to reappear

The planets' motion is choreographed to perfection
Their precise pattern hasn't changed since inception
It all fits together flawlessly like chapter and verse
Is there anything at all that's new in this Universe?

So where do I fit in, this small speck of history
If it's all master-planned, what's the plan for me?
Can I really accomplish anything; make a difference?
When my life is over, will it have any significance?

I've tried everything to find some bit of happiness
I thought it would come with business success
I loved that new car while it was shiny and in style
But the shine disappeared in just a short little while

I tried the proverbial wine, women, and song
But that too grew old and tiring before too long
My man-toys have all lost their charm and luster
None of it has been fulfilling or passed the muster

The man upstairs has quietly let me go my way
Knowing that I would have these questions someday
But lately, He's been speaking louder into both ears
That my focus has been misdirected all these years

You see, it was He who made me, and He has a plan
He's been counting on me ever since time began
To boldly proclaim His message to a lost generation
So all in my circle of influence receive revelation

There's a spiritual battle going on every day
And there's a part my Lord wants me to play
Go and make disciples of all nations is the call
And my part is significant to that effort after all

He sent His Son to provide meaning to my life
To find that meaning, all I had to do was accept Christ
I know what my purpose is, my mission to fulfill
It's to know my Lord and follow His will

I pray that I will be able to lead the life He wants me to
Knowing that only He can make all things new
So that when the Father comes to take me home
I'll know that the meaning in life comes from Him alone.

Your Story Matters

Jesus' instructions to His apostles were very clear
Go and make disciples of all the earth, far and near
This is what we're called to do, the Christian vision
But how do I do my part for the Great Commission?

I'm not a biblical scholar, and my memory's not very good
If I need to quote some pertinent verse, I'm not sure I could
My prayers are well-intended but often disjointed
If you're looking for Billy Graham, you'll be disappointed

But if you think back to those people God was able to use
They definitely were not the type to make the evening news
They were people like fishermen of ordinary skill and means
A willing teenager, a tax collector, and a shepherd boy extreme

Why wouldn't God have recruited a great orator or a king?
Someone who could captivate, add a measure of zing
I think it's because power is corrupting if it doesn't come from Him
And pride is one of the most difficult of the seven deadly sins

So you see, even with our limitations, we're a great asset
You won't know that until you see the table He's set
He'll provide you with the special connection you'll need
And do the rest of the work, if you just plant the seed

You have a unique story, and no one knows it better than you
And in the telling, what you have in common will come through
Bringing someone to Christ may be the ultimate end
But it all starts, first and foremost, with making a friend

Maybe your story will strengthen a faith that's weak
And it will be re-energized by the words you speak
God will be more than pleased from His throne on High
That, even with all your shortcomings, you gave it a try

In witnessing for Christ, don't try to be someone you're not
It won't matter what you remembered or what you forgot
God will provide, and you won't need biblical swagger
Just get started and know that your story matters.

ABOUT THE AUTHOR

Jim Tayburn grew up on a dairy farm in central New York State. Always knowing he wanted something more, he left that life behind to attend the University of Buffalo and never looked back. Out of college, he embarked on a thirty-seven-year career in sales and marketing with Occidental Petroleum, a job that took him and his wife, Marie, from Buffalo to Michigan, Missouri, Pennsylvania, and Arizona, where they currently live. While that may seem a little nomadic, Jim and Marie see it as a blessing because it allowed them to experience first-hand the cultural and geographic diversity of this great country. The Tayburns have two daughters, Lisa and Debbie, and three grandchildren, Jacob, Grace, and Emma, and if there's a downside to coming out West, it's that they all live in the East.

Jim has always had an ability for creative writing and thought the outlet for that would be as a novelist, but that never happened. God had a different plan. With the encouragement of friends and family, he began to write poetry, and his first book, *Lyrical Living*, was largely for them. As He often does when He opens a door, God has given Jim a new purpose in life. The result of his spiritual growth was his second book, *Growing in the Spirit*, which was aptly named. Jim's writing has continued, and he enjoys sharing in his poetry all that God has to offer for those who make a choice to follow "His Way."